Our Forever Angel

Surviving the Loss
of a Loved One to Suicide

By

Barb Scholz

ISBN: 1-4033-3247-9 (E-book)
ISBN: 1-4033-3248-7 (Paperback)
ISBN: 1-4033-3249-5 (Dustjacket)
ISBN: 1-4033-3250-9 (RocketBook)

Library of Congress Control Number: 2002092086

This book is printed on acid free paper.

Printed in the United States of America
Bloomington, IN

1st Books - rev. 07/29/02

Dedication

This book is dedicated to
my children,
Jon and Natasha.
You have been so strong and
mature through this difficult
time in your lives, and you
have ALWAYS been there for me.
You are the center of my universe!

In loving memory of Troy.

Contents

Acknowledgements

For Jon and Natasha, who I could not have gotten through this without. You have been the rock of my world since the day your dad died, and you have handled the situation with great poise and maturity. I could not be more proud of both of you, your accomplishments, and how you have grown through the difficult experience of losing your father at such an early age. I love you with all my heart! Thank you for being so supportive of my desire to write this book.

For the wonderful family support, from both Troy's and my own, I would like to say thanks! You were always there for me when I needed someone to talk to or cry with. Thank you to Mom and Dad who have always been there for me, Caroline who continues to treat me, Jon and Natasha exactly the same as she did before she lost her son. Thank you, Jay, for the long walk that first afternoon, a much needed breath of fresh air for me, Vickie (Chase and Brayden weren't with us yet), Ryan, who entertained us all during that long first day, Geri (Tim and Morgan weren't with us yet) who will always be one of my best friends, and Brian who was my rock through the first few weeks. Brian, you were the first person I called. I don't know how we would have gotten through it without you. You had the unpleasant task of calling to inform numerous family members, and you also stayed with us for several weeks until I felt comfortable enough to stay alone. Thank you, Brian, for being there for us, and for being such a great role model for Jon and Natasha! To the rest of Troy's family, who still include us in family get-togethers and treat us as members of the family. Grandma Benda, for treating us still as part of the family. Thank you, Todd, for the talk we had about me not taking the blame for what happened, Nicole, Cody and Connie. To Tary for not blaming me, Joe and Megan. To Kris for taking care of several details too difficult for me to take care of. To Tami who loved Troy very much but lives too far away for us to see as often as we would like. Thanks, Tracy, for telling me that I will always be a part of the Scholz family and for telling the kids that they will always be your niece and nephew. Thanks for always treating us that way and for helping me with the kids when I need to be out of town. Thanks, also, for just being a friend. Thanks to Ray, Connie, Cayce, Lynae and Emily for always treating us as part of the family and for helping me so much with Jon and Natasha. Special thanks to Ray for taking Jon to the father/son breakfast for

vii

several years since he lost his dad. And to every other family member who has shown care and concern for our well-being.

Thank you, Linda, for helping me through the initial shock, for helping with Jon and Natasha while I explained to each of them what happened, and for taking charge until family arrived.

I would also like to thank St. Isidore's school staff for taking such good care of Jon and Natasha when I was not able to be right by their side to protect them. You handled the entire situation in a very positive manner, and through your efforts, neither Jon nor Natasha ever came home from school upset over something hurtful that another child in their class said or did. This is quite an amazing accomplishment, considering that kids, even if unintentional, can be very honest and hurtful with their words at times. Thank you to the entire St. Isidore's school staff!

I would like to thank Dr. Ross Pilkington for reading and critiquing my work and for providing feedback. Much of the supporting material from a counseling perspective comes from him, as well as many insights into what I wrote. Thanks also for the encouraging words along the way that kept me believing that what I was doing would be helpful to other people when all was said and done. You provided me the inspiration and constant encouragement that I needed to keep my excitement about what I was doing at an ultimate high. Your compliments and encouragement kept me from doubting the value and worth of my work.

Thank you to Denise Carlson of the Methodist Employee Assistance Program for giving me Dr. Pilkington's name for a potential reviewer of my work. Also for the great information you shared in your presentation that I was able to include.

Thank you to Barb Wheeler for sharing many experiences from her years of work counseling people who were suicidal, as well as people who had lost a family member to suicide. Also to Harold Wheeler for sharing experiences of how he has been touched by suicide.

Much of the "advice" I will share are actually words of wisdom from two wonderful counselors. Karen Kelly, who was the counselor I went to myself, and Deb Stranberg, who was the counselor at Jon and Natasha's school at the time of Troy's death. I would like to thank both of these amazing women for their assistance in helping me and my children get back on the right track and deal with this loss in a healthy manner.

Thank you to Ella Robinson for her editing skills, and to Jeanne Schieffer who reviewed my writing and provided guidance in helping me develop this book into a more complete work.

And last, but certainly not least, I would like to thank all of my wonderful friends who were there for me when I needed them. Thanks to Amy who always checked up on me to see how I was doing and was always willing to listen when I needed someone to talk to or cry with. Thanks to Lori, Colleen and Cola, who numerous times listened to me "unload" when I was having a bad day, as we went walking on our break at work. To Lori, Carla and Jill, who I promised while I shared the idea of the book with them that I would mention them! They are also great friends who were there to listen when I needed them. To Caree who kept encouraging me to write this book even when I didn't think I could do it. To Carolyn, for her encouragement before and during my work.

And to all of my other friends who provided words of comfort or encouragement. Thankfully, for me, there are too many of you to mention because I would hate to leave anybody out, but you know who you are!

Preface

Before I begin, I would like to explain why I wrote this book. When I first approached my supervisor about the possibility of temporarily working in a part-time status in order to do this, I told him, "I have a very specific message I would like to share. I would like to be able to help other people get through similar experiences to what I have now been through."

I would like to make it very clear that there are NO intentions to place any blame, point any fingers, or cause any additional pain to anyone for what has happened. The sole purpose of this book is to reach out and help other people. Suicide is oftentimes something that is kept in the closet. It is not a subject people talk about openly, the way they might if someone died of cancer or a heart attack. It is simply not a socially acceptable death. People will talk about it, but usually in more of a destructive manner than a constructive one. The people who talk about it are the ones who are speculating as to what happened and why, with no concern for the loved ones left behind who are suffering. But it is a difficult subject for people to talk about with those who ARE suffering; so, many times, people say nothing. This may leave the loved ones feeling helpless, with nowhere to turn and nobody to talk to who REALLY understands what they are experiencing.

Thus, the reason for the book. I wish there would never again be a reason for a book of this sort, because I wish nobody had to go through this difficult experience. But, the sad fact is, suicide DOES happen, and therefore, people need ways to try to understand it and to deal with it. If I can help ease the pain in any possible way for other people, then I will have met my objective.

Although I will share many stories about my experience, I have also tried to get other perspectives. Every suicide that happens has different circumstances; so, by no means do I assume that everyone's experience is the same as what mine was. However, I believe that many of the feelings are probably similar. I would like to offer something in this book for various situations in order to touch as many people as possible. It is my sincere wish that I be able to help every person who reads this book in some way or another.

Chapter 1

The Initial Shock

When You Receive The News

It was 10:00 Saturday morning, January 14, 1995. When my husband, Troy, left that morning, it was with the understanding that we were separating. Several years earlier, when our marital problems became obvious, he told me he had almost killed himself. I looked at him in total disbelief and asked, "Even if you hated me, how could you do that to the kids?" He responded, "Why do you think I'm still here?" From the minute he made that comment, I felt pretty confident that even though he might contemplate suicide, he would never actually go through with it.

After he left that morning, the kids and I packed our bags to stay with my sister for the weekend, but Jon and Natasha wanted to play a board game before we left. I'm not sure why I agreed to play, because I was rather anxious to get out of town, but I did. It was fortunate that we played that game, because otherwise we would have been on the road to my sister's house. As it turned out, we had just finished the game and were putting things away when the doorbell rang. As I walked toward the door, I saw a police officer. A feeling of numbness passed through every inch of my body, as I knew something was terribly wrong.

Linda, the wife of my husband's employer came with the officer to tell me the news. She nicely asked Jon and Natasha to go upstairs to their rooms to play for a little while. Once they were out of ear's range, the police officer proceeded to tell me that my husband, Troy, had been found earlier that morning with a single gunshot wound to the head, apparently self-inflicted. I dropped down on the couch, my body as lifeless as a rag doll. I do not remember what the officer said after that. I couldn't hear him over my sobbing, "No, no, no!" And at that point I did not care what else he had to say. My heart felt like it had swelled to ten times its' normal size, and my throat as if it could explode at any minute, as I wrapped my arms tightly around myself while I cried.

1

Then suddenly I had a feeling of urgency. Reality had not set in yet. I thought to myself, "I know First Aid and CPR... if I hurry, I can save him." The officer had not actually said that the gunshot wound had killed him. Surely, I thought, he must still be alive. You see, somehow, this HAD to be reversible!

I couldn't believe it when they told me he was gone. Just a few short hours earlier he was talking to his kids, and now he was dead... it was over. There was no reversing this one.

Once I realized it was too late, that he was definitely gone, I began sobbing again. I felt responsible for his death. Yes, we were having marital problems that I could no longer deal with, and yes, I had told him so that morning, but the last thing in the world I wanted was for him to die because of it. Even though I no longer loved him the way a wife loves a husband, as I had told him before he died, I will always love him as the good person that he was.

"Love is when you take away the feeling, the passion, the romance and you find out you still love the person."

- Author Unknown

The police officer didn't stay long. He just told me the news and then left. I thank God to this day that he sent Linda with the police officer. She comforted and consoled me, and then helped me gain my composure enough to be able to explain this to my children, Jon who was eight years old at the time, and Natasha who was six.

I had not yet moved from the spot on the couch I had fell onto when the police officer told me the news. I wiped the tears from my eyes and face and took several very deep breaths. I was as ready as anyone could ever be to tell their children that their Daddy had died. Linda brought Jon to me first and kept Natasha busy while I sat Jon on the couch and talked to him. Then she kept Jon busy while I talked to Natasha. I explained to each of them individually that Daddy was now in heaven with Grandpa, and that he would be the best guardian angel for us that anyone could ever have. I never actually told them Daddy had died, which may not have been the best approach. I should have probably told them he was dead so there would be no confusion about that fact, but I just could not bear to say those words yet. I knew I would break down and start crying again if I said *died* or *dead*, and I wanted to be strong for the kids. I was also trying to soften the blow and make it a little easier for them. Natasha cried only briefly, as she did not really understand what had happened. Jon cried a little more, but he did not fully understand either. They both probably cried more because they saw how upset I was than because they understood what was happening.

After a short while, another police officer came to my house. He said he had to ask me some routine questions about what happened. He started by asking if I knew why Troy might do something like this. When I told him we had been having marital problems, he began poking and prodding with numerous questions about it until I fought back. "It feels like you are accusing me of killing him," I said.

"I'm sorry," he responded. "I have to do this." He again told me that it was all just routine. My emotions quickly went from sadness and devastation to anger and defensiveness as I explained the facts to the officer.

I'm sure the officer was just doing his job, but I could not believe the questions he was asking me. I know he needed to make sure that I had not pulled the trigger and set it up to look like a suicide, but I hadn't even had time to grieve yet, and here I was, feeling like I was on trial for my husband's death. I had visions of defending myself in court even before I had a chance to think about planning a funeral! Finally, he was satisfied with the answers, and he left.

At that point, Linda asked if there was anyone I would like to have her call. I asked her to call my brother, Brian, who lived in town. He immediately rushed over. Linda stopped him at the back door to the house, and as she shared the news with him in the kitchen about what happened, I could hear the heavy sigh as he said, "Oh, no!" I was still sitting on the couch in the living room. I couldn't find the strength to stand up yet. I felt numb and light-headed, like all of the blood had flushed out of my body as I listened to her tell Brian the news. I felt the numb feeling numerous times that day… every time the news was shared with someone new I felt that light-headedness all over again. After Linda told Brian what happened, she quietly slipped away to allow him to take over. He took on the unpleasant task of calling family members to let them know what had happened and to ask them to come as soon as possible. Before he got a chance to call Troy's mother and grandmother, they showed up at our house. They happened to be in town to do some shopping and decided to stop by. Luckily, they did not go to the store where Troy worked, because that was where he had chosen to die. It would have been devastating for them to show up there with police officers investigating his death.

Brian called our mom and dad and told them I needed to see them right away. When they arrived, he shared the news with them. Again, the feeling of numbness came over me. They were in total shock. They had no idea we were having marital problems, because I had wanted to protect them from the pain over the years. They felt terrible that they had not been able to be of any help to us while we were struggling, but that had been my choice. When Brian called our sister, Geri, he simply said I needed her to come as soon as possible. She had a 1½-hour drive, and he did not want her to drive that distance shocked and upset, so he did not tell her what happened until she arrived at the house. I had confided in Geri about the problems Troy and I were having, so our separation wouldn't have been a surprise. Troy's death, on the other hand, was a total shock.

He called our other brother Jay and told him what happened, as he knew with his job and family, Jay needed to know how important it was that they come right away. When they arrived, Jay and I went out for a walk around the block, which was the first daylight I had seen since receiving the news. I remember wondering if the people who saw us walking knew what had happened. But since it had not hit the local newspaper yet, I think very few people would have, only those who had heard about it by word of mouth.

My friend, Amy, called that night. She had been out of town for the day and had several messages on her answering machine saying that she needed to call me. None of the messages actually said what happened, just that she needed to call me. Amy knew that Troy and I were having marital problems, and there was a good chance we would be separating. When she called, she asked if everything was OK, and I started to cry as I told her no, everything was not OK.

She asked me, "What did he do, kill himself?" I said, "Yes, he did." I don't think she believed me at first, but it became apparent very quickly that I was serious about what I was telling her. We talked for a while, and she and another friend, Carla, stopped by the house a little later to express their sympathies in person.

Every time someone new arrived, I cried all over again. I was in total shock and disbelief. I could not believe he had actually gone through with it. And yet when our marriage finally got to the point of separation, and I saw the police officer at my door, somehow I knew what had happened.

Even though I had the facts about what happened, it was difficult to believe it was actually true. I wanted to know when we could see him. The mortician said it wouldn't be a good idea until they had fully prepared him. So we scheduled a time on Sunday, the day after Troy died, for the family to meet at the mortuary to make the funeral arrangements. Sunday was also Troy's mom's birthday, and I remember thinking, "What a way to spend your birthday, making funeral arrangements for your 32-year-old son." After the questions had been answered concerning flowers, the casket, obituary, cemetery, and many others, I again asked if we could see Troy, but they said he still wasn't ready. The mortician told me if we saw him before he was fully prepared, it would be a "stark" site. So again, we waited.

It wasn't until Monday that we were allowed to view the body. This seemed like the longest two days of my life. Until we saw him, it didn't seem real. It felt like this was all just a very bad dream, and that any minute I would wake up to find out it wasn't really happening. Once we could see him with our own eyes it became real... he was gone.

At times during those first few days, I felt like I was living in a vacuum. The world was moving around me, but I didn't feel like I was moving with it. Conversations were muffled like I was under water, and even though I could hear them, it sounded as though the people talking were miles away when they were right next to me. I was in another world. I felt guilty attending the services as Troy's grieving wife, knowing I had prompted his suicide because of the separation that he did not want, but I did.

The "family viewing" was prior to opening the doors of the mortuary for visitors. My first thought when I saw him was that his hair didn't look at all the way he had fixed it. It was combed straight down on his forehead. Troy always combed it to the side. I asked the mortician to comb his hair more to the side so it would look more like him. He adjusted it a little, but not much. Although the police officer had told me Troy had died from a gunshot wound, he had not told me exactly how he shot himself, and I had never asked. It was not until several days later that my sister-in-law told me there was a bullet wound on his forehead, and that was the reason his hair had been combed the way it was, to cover the wound.

During the visitation at the mortuary, several of the teachers from Jon and Natasha's school came to visit. Natasha's teacher said she hoped I would be able to keep the kids at St. Isidore's. I knew it was a very good school, but now we would struggle to pay the tuition. Ever since this happened to us, however, I never had another thought about moving them from St. Isidore's. I could not have asked for the school to handle it any better than they did. They were absolutely wonderful about the entire situation. They were very positive and never looked on our situation in a negative light.

That evening there would be a Rosary, or prayer service, for him. I was overwhelmed by all of the people who attended. There were people from all facets of Troy's life, as well as mine, Jon's and Natasha's. At the suggestion of Troy's brother, Todd, one of Troy's favorite songs, "Time in a Bottle" by Jim Croce, was played at the end of the service. This brought tears to everyone's eyes, especially those closest to Troy who knew how special that song was to him and how much he loved Jim Croce.

The priest who conducted the service eluded that Troy would not be allowed into heaven because of what he did. I do not remember the exact words, and he did not come right out and say it, but that was the message many people heard. It upset several of the family members, and someone confronted him about it. Following the prayer service, lots of people came to the house. It was comforting, being surrounded by so many people who cared.

Tuesday morning for the funeral service, the family arrived at the church early in order to have our final viewing of Troy's body. Once the casket was closed, we would never see him again. We said our final good-byes, and then waited behind closed curtains for people to arrive and fill up the church.

Again, I was overwhelmed at the number of people who came to express sympathy to the family over Troy's death. The eulogy was delivered by a young priest, Fr. Jim Meysenburg. I had graduated from high school with Jim, and he had grown up with Troy in the small town of 300 people where the funeral was being held. They had played baseball and other sports together since they were little boys. He did a wonderful job expressing how Troy would have never hurt anyone intentionally, which was true. He had a difficult time getting through his eulogy without choking over his own words, but it was very personal, very touching and meaningful to the family. He jointly celebrated the funeral mass with the priest who had conducted the Rosary service the night before.

During the funeral, the priest who had upset the family at the prayer service the night before made amends with the family. As part of a Catholic mass, there is a Sign of Peace, where you turn to your neighbors, shake their hand and offer your peace to them. At this time in the mass, the priest who had conducted the Rosary the night before, and unbeknownst to him had upset the family, came over to the family, offered them peace and apologized for upsetting us. Evidently his words did not come out quite the way he had meant them to, and he said that the church had changed its viewpoint on suicide and the possibility of still being allowed into heaven.

The Catholic Church believes the taking of a human life is a mortal sin, and that if the person had not confessed and felt truly sorry for having done so, they would not have the privilege of heaven. This would include the taking of your own life. At one time, people who committed suicide were not allowed to have funeral services through the church or to be buried in a Catholic cemetery. This added a tremendous burden to the grieving family who were already mourning the death of their loved one. Fortunately, with a better understanding of psychology and depression as a mental illness, the church has changed its views on suicide. The person can now have a Catholic funeral and be buried in a Catholic cemetery. The belief today is that the person still does have the opportunity to go to heaven.

After the funeral, we drove to the cemetery for the burial. The cemetery Troy was buried in was in another small town, approximately 20 miles away; so, he could be laid to rest with his father, who had gone before him, and where some day, his mother will join both of them. There were so many cars in the funeral procession that it went for miles. My memory of the actual burial ceremony is almost blank. I remember arriving at the cemetery, getting out of the car and walking with Jon and Natasha to the tent surrounding the plot where he would be laid to rest. I felt numb, like it wasn't really happening. I don't remember much more than that, other than the fact that it was cold and the wind was blowing. The cemetery where he was laid to rest is at the top of a hill with no trees for protection, so it always seems that it is colder there than anywhere else.

Once the burial ceremony was complete, there was a dinner at the church. Already, I was feeling better. There really is truth to the fact that the funeral is part of the healing process and closure. After the funeral was over, we could start thinking about going on with our lives. I talked to many, many people at the dinner who came to express their sympathy. The last people to leave were a group of my high school friends. Some of them I had not seen in several years, and it was great to see them again. We reminisced about things we had done in high school. We talked and we laughed. We laughed until we cried. It was the most therapeutic thing I could have done that day.

Meanwhile, several of Troy's high school friends had stayed in town for some socializing as well. It would have been nice to join them, and I had been invited to, but it wasn't appropriate. When it was time for my friends to leave, I went back to Troy's mom's house where several of the relatives had gathered. We went through the memorial cards and the guest books signed by visitors, family and friends. There had been so many people in those several days that I didn't see everyone. Some of the people who signed the books I didn't know, so Troy's mom and grandma and my mom filled me in if I did not know the person. Some of them, none of us knew, so we concluded that they were friends of Troy's through work.

In the casket with Troy, the florist had included a white pillow outlined with lace and decorated with a floral arrangement. The arrangement included two artificial red roses with greenery and a gold ribbon, three live red roses with greenery and baby's breath, and a red ribbon. It was meant to be from Jon and Natasha. I had forgotten about this arrangement until months later when I saw the pillow on the shelf in Natasha's closet. The morticians must have removed it prior to the burial. I don't know how Natasha got her hands on it, but I am glad she did. She still keeps it in her room years later. In fact, one day when I had her clean her room, I noticed she had tied a string to the back of the pillow so she could hang it on her wall.

She also has his favorite baseball cap. Troy was a loyal Phillies fan, even when they were not doing very well. He wore his Phillies cap around the house all the time. After he died, Natasha would wear this cap around the house at times. Anything she could do to make herself feel closer to her dad, she did. She has now retired the cap, though, as at the same time she hung the pillow on her wall, she hung his Phillies cap next to it. She created her own little memorial for her dad right next to her bed.

She has since also hung a basket where the dried petals from the live roses on the pillow rest in the bottom, and Troy's picture stands behind them. I thought she might be afraid that this memorial would cause her friends to ask questions, but she is not. She is as proud as can be of the memorial she created for her dad.

Jon and Natasha wanted to go back to school the day after the funeral, and they seemed to me to be doing as well as could be expected, so I was going to send them. Then I got scared that maybe they weren't really ready, so I called the school. The counselor from their school made a personal visit to our house and talked to each of the kids separately to give me her assessment of how she thought they were doing. After talking with them, she told me she thought they were doing fine, and that they were ready to go back to school, so they went back in the afternoon.

Mrs. Stranberg was a wonderful counselor. Before the kids returned to school, she went to every single classroom in the school, which included 14 classrooms, and talked to the kids about how to act around Jon and Natasha concerning their dad's death. She could have easily stopped at talking only to their individual classes, but instead she talked to every class in the school.

I am confident this is why neither Jon nor Natasha ever had a hurtful incident at school related to Troy's death.

By now, everyone else had gone back to daily life. But there was still some business that had to be taken care of. Troy had driven his van to work that Saturday morning, which was where he decided to take his life. I thank God that he did not choose to do it at home. I'm sure it would have been much more difficult for us if either of the kids or I would have found him, or if we would have seen him that way.

His van was filled with fishing poles, tools and racks that had been there ever since Troy's dad used the van for his electrician and plumbing business. Someone needed to clean out the van. I wanted to sell it because the memories associated with it were too painful. I didn't have the strength to clean it out. It was too hard for me. I did not even want to SEE the van, much less go inside and clean it out! Luckily, my sister-in-law at the time, Kris, offered to do it for me. I did not really care about the value of any of the items in the van. I just wanted someone to get rid of things so I would not have to see them ever again. It was just too difficult.

He also had numerous tools where he worked, which he had purchased himself. I never got them back. It was too difficult for me to go back to the store where he installed and serviced car stereos. This being where he actually died, it was too hard to go back there, besides the fact that I would not have known which tools he had purchased and which ones he had not.

Someone also needed to go through all of his clothes in the dresser and closet. At the time, it sent chills down my spine just walking on his side of the bed, much less actually going through all of his clothes. But I knew the sooner I got rid of some of those things, the sooner I could start moving on with my life, since I would not have the constant reminders surrounding me. Again, I was lucky to have someone offer to help me. My friend Amy offered to come over and go through his clothes with me so I could take them to the Goodwill. Her help made this task much easier to bear.

Just a few days after Troy's funeral, a good friend's mother passed away. It was too soon after his funeral for me to deal with attending this one. I just was not ready yet. But I will always remember the first funeral I went to after Troy's. Several months later, another good friend who had battled with cancer for several years finally lost the fight and died. Although it was difficult to go to a funeral, I went out of respect for my friend. The ceremony was very different than Troy's since it was in a different type of church, but still the memories were there. We had chosen some traditional funeral songs, such as "How Great Thou Art" and "Amazing Grace," so of course, I hear these songs regularly when I attend funerals. It still brings back memories of Troy's funeral when I hear those songs, and I still choke back tears when I sing them.

The facts were clear — Troy was gone and he had committed suicide. I still, for the first year, thought about it in disbelief every day. It was on my mind at all times. I could not even imagine life ever being so bad that I would get to the point of suicide, or having absolutely no hope for the future that things would get better and eventually be OK again. That was one of the fundamental differences between Troy and me.

However, after Troy's death, there would be days at work, when for no apparent reason, I would find myself blankly staring into nothingness. I could not function. I couldn't force myself to do any work or even focus on my computer's monitor to read an e-mail message. Sounds were muffled around me again. I was totally incapacitated. The hardest thing about this was that many times when it happened, nothing had taken place to trigger it—at least nothing I could identify. I would be working away, when it would hit me as if someone had shot me with a stun gun. When this happened, I would just sit back in my chair, holding back the tears while I stared into space.

Luckily for me, I had some great friends who I went for walks with on work breaks. It was all I could do to focus on the buttons of the telephone to dial one of their phone numbers and say, "I need a break." Normally, we had certain times of the day when we went on break, but without fail, if I would call, and my friend could tell that I really needed to take a break, she dropped whatever she was working on and we went for a walk. Some days I needed to unload something that was bothering me. Other days I needed to cry. And sometimes, I just needed a friend to walk by my side or to give me a hug. I knew I could always count on my friends to be there for whatever I needed at the time.

I would not be where I am today if not for the help and understanding of many great friends who were there for me. I strongly suggest that anyone who is struggling with something in their lives find someone who provides that outlet for them. Whether it is good friends; a family member; a counselor; a priest, minister or other church staff member, it does not matter as long as you have some way to let your feelings go when you need to. Don't try to be strong enough to get through this on your own. Asking for help does not make you weak. When you get lost, you ask for directions, and this is no different. You can get through it on your own, but it will probably take a lot more time and effort to get back to normal again. When people offer to help, they are sincere. Don't turn them away. Tell them thank you and accept their help.

Suicide is not an easy thing to deal with. There are a lot of emotions and questions to try to understand. It is much easier with the help of others.

In this book, I've included information from many different resources. There are inspirational quotes I received via e-mail or heard in presentations. There is a wealth of information from Dr. Ross Pilkington, who critiqued my work and gave me feedback on my writing. I also received a lot of information from the Methodist Employee Assistance Program, which I found to be helpful and have included it. This information is included and the book is more than my story so that it can help people. Not only do I find this information to be helpful, but I hope this also sends the message that we need to keep our eyes and ears open, looking for resources to help us rather than thinking we can handle it alone. By no means do I claim to be the originator of any of this information. It is included to add value to the book and to anyone reading it.

When I began writing, I realized that in the years since Troy died, I had lost touch with several of the people who helped us on our road to recovery. One of those people was the counselor at Jon and Natasha's school when Troy died. I contacted her to see if she had any stories she might like to share in the book, and several weeks later she wrote me a letter. In the letter she says, "I have observed the effects of suicide on families in three situations, and I guess, the unfinished business is what I observed to be so devastating for these families. The anger, hurt, and complete sadness of not finishing what life offers."

The "unfinished business" of daily activities, such as going through clothes, cleaning out vehicles, and so forth, is difficult for those left behind to take care of in the case of any death. But Mrs. Stranberg relates to the much deeper issue of "not finishing what life offers." The person will never get to give their children and grandchildren a hug again, never get to go for a picnic or a walk on the beach with loved ones again, never have the opportunity to say "I love you!" again, and never get to accomplish the dreams they had in life.

I still, at times, years later, sit and think in amazement about what happened and have a hard time believing that it is true. But, as with a lot of the emotions and reactions you have as you deal with a suicide, or any tragic event in your life, this too, gets easier with time. Now, instead of thinking about it every day, I may think about it in disbelief once a week, or every other week. I will probably always have a hard time believing that this has really happened, but at least now it does not consume my every thought throughout the day.

The Stages of Grief

Although I did not realize it at the time, what I was experiencing was all very normal. When I struggled with believing Troy had actually committed suicide, I was in the "Denial" stage in the process of grieving, according to Swiss-born psychiatrist Dr. Elisabeth Kubler-Ross. Dr. Kubler-Ross has counseled hundreds of people through her research into death and dying and has written many books, including *On Death and Dying*. She describes the five classic stages of grief that are very common for people to experience. There are many different philosophies on grief stages by different researchers, but I will use those studied by Dr. Kubler-Ross.

Denial/Disbelief – Upon hearing the news of a loved one's death, it is common to react with shock or disbelief. According to Dr. Kubler-Ross, this is a healthy stage, which permits you to develop other defenses. During this stage, thoughts of "It did not happen" or "It could not have happened" may go through your head. This stage is usually short-lived. Reality usually sets in fairly quickly.

For me, however, this stage was not short-lived. This stage is probably normally longer in the case of a suicide since it is so difficult to comprehend that it actually happened.

Anger or resentment – "Why my child?" or "Why did this have to happen?" are common questions to ask in this stage. Blame directed at the person who has died, at yourself, at someone you may feel was a factor in the death, or even God, is often part of this stage. This is also a very normal feeling and should be allowed to be experienced, as long as it is done in a constructive manner and not to hurt someone else. If the anger grows and is not dealt with, it becomes out of control. We need to process our anger so we can move on to the next stage. This may require help to learn how to process the anger properly.

Bargaining/Compromise/Negotiation – This is the self-talk and thinking we do to offer ourselves HOPE. "If everyone else stays healthy,

..." "If I can find another relationship, ..." "When I get better, ..." are common thoughts during this stage. Dr. Kubler-Ross calls this a period of temporary truce.

Depression/Sadness - Now with the courage to admit what has happened, the acknowledgment of what has happened brings depression. Although this is very difficult to go through, we must do it. You cannot cut it out of the process of healing. During this stage, we may need "support counseling."

Acceptance – At last! You are free again! This is a time of facing the loss calmly and accepting it, in order to go on with your life. At this point, you can talk about your loss without sadness and tears. You can remember the good times spent with your lost loved one. Life is going on, you are comfortable again and are fully functioning.

According to the counseling profession, although there are many theories about the stages of grief, there seems to be a commonality in all theories. There is some period of Avoidance of the loss, followed by a Confrontation of the feelings being experienced, and finally a Reorganization of life. The important thing to remember about these stages of grief is that each of them is normal to experience, but you need to allow yourself to experience the feelings you are having rather than ignore them. For me, just knowing what was normal, and what to expect, was comforting and helped me get through the loss easier. As stated by Dr. Pilkington, "If you recognize the signs of the stages of grief, you can keep track of what stage you are in and monitor your progress. You may advance and fall back, but as long as there is a plan and you know where you are, you will know where you need to go. This will help you not feel lost since you are recovering via five stages."

"These stages of grief can be experienced after a death, after a divorce, after learning of a terminal illness, or any other type of loss. A loss is a loss, is a loss. People experiencing grief of any type need to be able to see a light at the end of the tunnel rather than a train. Understanding these stages of grief offers us evidence of progress, hope and encouragement that things will get better once we reach that stage of Acceptance." says Dr. Pilkington.

Throughout the chapters of this book I will refer to Dr. Kubler-Ross's stages of grief, but especially in Chapter 9, "Is there such a thing as 'proper' and 'improper' grieving? Everyone Grieves Differently, So Nobody Can Tell You How."

Natasha Sleeping in My Bed

The day Troy died was obviously a very long day for all of us. Someone had suggested to me that I call my doctor and get a prescription for some sleeping pills to help me get some rest. I really did not like the thought of taking sleeping pills, and I definitely did not want to start something that I was going to have a hard time stopping later. Besides, I thought, I was so exhausted from the day, that I would not have any trouble sleeping. But when it came time to go to bed, it was difficult to think about sleeping in the bed Troy had slept in less than 24 hours earlier. Just knowing that he was not alive to be able to sleep in any bed made it hard to even look at "his side" of the bed. It was a very long time before I could even walk on "his side" of the bed without getting chills.

The first night after he died, I was sure that Natasha needed a little extra security. So I asked if she would like me to sleep in her bed with her. I said if she would be more comfortable, I would sleep with her, but in reality, it was ME who needed the extra security that night. I had not been without another adult in a house overnight much, since I went straight from high school and living at home to college with roommates. Troy and I had gotten married very shortly after I graduated from college, so I was not comfortable staying alone overnight.

When I thought about it, though, that couldn't have been the problem, because I had someone staying at the house with us for at least two or three weeks after Troy died. My mom and dad stayed several days, my sister stayed several days, and my brother stayed a week or two until I finally felt comfortable without anyone else but me and the kids in the house. Still, it was me who did not want to sleep in my bed alone. What was I afraid of? Looking back, I think it was more the thought of sleeping in the bed that was Troy's and mine together. Sleeping in Natasha's bed was a crutch I used at the time, a security blanket, and it became quite comforting for both of us.

Eventually, we moved to my bed since it was a king-sized waterbed with a lot more room than her bed. I made Natasha sleep on Troy's side of the bed, which she gladly did, as I hugged the railing on my side. Finally, after several months of this, I realized it was time for it to stop. I was comfortable enough to sleep in my bed by myself, and it was a habit that needed to be broken before she got any older. Natasha and I talked about the need for her to go back to her own bed, but it was a hard habit to break.

That fall, I came up with a solution. I asked Natasha if she would sleep in her own bed again if I got her a waterbed for Christmas. She seemed excited about this and said she would, so that was the plan. Jon and Natasha each received a waterbed for Christmas that first year, and that is how we broke the habit of her sleeping in my bed.

You Didn't Know How Much You Were Loved

"When you were born, you were crying and everyone around you was smiling. Live your life so that when you die, you're smiling and everyone around you is crying ~ tears of joy for having known you."

Author Unknown

I really do not think Troy realized how many people cared about him and missed him when he died. He was a good person who would have helped anyone who was in need. He simply did not know how to help himself. I hope he watched down the night of his rosary and the day of his funeral to see both buildings bursting at the seams with so many people they could not hold them all. This was a tribute to Troy and the good person that he was.

Chapter 2

Why???

The Most Difficult Question to Answer Following a Suicide

How could Troy, who supposedly loved us so much, willingly hurt us so deeply? Searching for the answer to the never-ending question of "Why?" he committed suicide was one of the most difficult aspects of dealing with it. Coping with the initial shock and disbelief was difficult, but even after getting past that, I had a difficult time understanding WHY he did what he did. The best definition I have heard for suicide is that it is a "permanent solution to a temporary problem." As mentioned earlier, I could never imagine my life being so bad that I would get to the point of ending it. So, it was difficult for me to comprehend Troy wanting to end his. Until you know some of the underlying reasons, it is difficult to get through the healing process. Once you recognize the motivation for the suicide, you can start developing solutions.

Probably the best thing I did for myself through this entire experience was to get in touch with a professional counselor. I did this almost immediately following Troy's death, and I really believe it helped me through the recovery process to be much healthier and to recover more quickly than if I had not done so.

My counselor, Karen Kelly, helped me identify with underlying causes better than I ever could have figured them out on my own. Today, I think I empathize with what Troy did as much as I will ever be able to. In order for me to be fully aware of the state of mind and the desperation he must have felt at that moment, I think I would have to be capable of doing the same myself. So with that in mind, I hope I NEVER fully grasp why. But Karen helped tremendously in my comprehension of what Troy did. I realize that not every situation is exactly like what I went through, but I think there are common denominators in every suicide that can be recognized.

Suicide knows no social, racial or economic boundaries. One thing my counselor told me is a very common factor, however, is a low level of self-esteem. I had realized for years that Troy had a problem with self-esteem, but there were a lot of things about it that I did not understand. First of all, I had no idea it could cause him to lose hope to the point that he could take his own life over it.

Troy and I had gone to high school in the same town, but at different schools. I knew who he was, and he knew who I was all through those years, but we didn't start dating until midway through our senior year. He was very athletic, handsome, and had numerous girls pursuing him, so from an outsider's view he appeared to be on top of the world. He seemed to have everything any high school teenage boy could want. I was surprised, and actually honored that he would be interested in me in the slightest way. That's why it was so shocking to get to know Troy, and to find out that deep down inside, he was lacking in self-confidence.

He was epileptic which could have been a very difficult and embarrassing thing for a teenager to deal with, but he handled it very well. He was extremely open about it and had no problem talking about the epilepsy. His openness made it easier for me to admit to people that he had it.

However, he was exceptionally self-conscious of his hair loss. His anxiety about the hair loss made it uncomfortable for me as well. When others would tease him about it, he was exceedingly sensitive, so I never mentioned it around him. The fact that we couldn't talk about it openly made it awkward for both of us. I think it was an enormous reason for his lack of self-confidence. I can remember him calling himself "ugly looking."

During my writing, Dr. Pilkington sent me an audiotape reading of the book *Celebrate the Sun*. The very powerful story was about how we place too much emphasis on always being the best at everything and the stress that puts on people. I think this is a very common problem in today's world. Everyone pushes so hard to get the best job with the best pay and the best title, which are faulty life goals. Sometimes we forget what is really important in life. We can also put too much pressure on others to be the best or to be like we are.

"To love is to let those we love be perfectly themselves and not to twist them with our own image. Otherwise, we love only the reflection of ourselves we find in them."

- Author Unknown

17

I recently watched an episode of the TV show *Touched By an Angel*. The show was about a man who just turned 40 and appeared to have everything going for him in life. He had a beautiful wife, a wonderful son, and was doing quite well in his farming business. Just when everything seemed to be going great for him, he committed suicide. His wife was very angry and bitter, and she was desperately searching for reasons why. In her desperation, she lashed out at everyone around her, indicating that somehow they were to blame. She was oblivious to her son's denial of what happened. All he could think or talk about was the calf in the barn, which was fighting for its life, but she did not care about the calf or her son's concern for it. She was too consumed by her own grief.

After the angel, Andrew, helped her understand what had happened with her husband and why, she explained it to her son. She told him that everyone loses hope at certain points in their life, but that most of us are able to find that hope again. His daddy had lost hope for one second, and then another, and another, until he just could not find any hope left any more.

I think that was an excellent explanation of how someone must feel right before they commit suicide. They must not be able to envision any small morsel of hope left in their lives to make it worth living, and they probably think the world will be better off without them. I believe it is a sort of "temporary insanity."

Although this may not be true in all cases, one possible explanation came from my kids' counselor at school. She told me that eventually Jon and Natasha would need to understand that their dad died because of a mental illness. Many people die of heart disease, cancer, or other illnesses, and their dad had an illness too, which he could not overcome on his own.

Another thing I did not understand about Troy's problems with self-esteem was that they were not caused by me or by anything I had done. I had always referred to his low self-esteem as insecurity, which I had blamed myself for, ever since we got married.

I had graduated from a technical school with a degree in Computer Programming, and therefore, had a very good paying job, with opportunities for advancement and a career. He had dropped out of college when he was very near graduation, over a disagreement with one of the college staff. He worked in a music store, selling and installing car stereo equipment. He thoroughly enjoyed what he did and was very good at it. He especially took pleasure in working with the young kids, who were his most frequent customers. He liked talking to the kids who were less popular or those who were considered to be "different" than the other kids. He found fulfillment in helping these kids feel better about themselves, and he believed that he could make a difference in their lives. He was an extremely caring person.

The people whose lives he touched were the most important thing to him. Money was less important, but it still bothered him that I made significantly more money than he did. He was brought up to believe that the man was to be the breadwinner. I think he felt that he wasn't fulfilling his role as the provider for the family since I made more money. Even though it wasn't my fault, I felt guilty that I had taken this perceived responsibility away from him.

I also played softball, volleyball, racquetball, and other sports, so I had made a lot of friends through these activities. This was threatening to him. His perpetual jealousy had him constantly worrying that I would meet someone who would take me away from him, even though whenever I played sports, I would play the game and come straight home. I never socialized with the team after the games, because when I did, he would be even more jealous and suspicious of what I was doing and who I was with. Although he had lots of friends through work, and was very well liked, he preferred to come home at night and stay there. If he wanted to do anything in his free time, it was to go fishing where he could just relax and get away from other stresses in his life. He was content to sit on the bank of a pond or river and never get a bite. I didn't mind going fishing, but I would get bored with it very quickly if we weren't catching any fish. His friends were different than my friends, and he wasn't comfortable socializing with my friends, so the only socializing I did was at my sporting activities.

I knew that Troy was insecure, so I tried to do everything I could when we first got married to minimize that insecurity. For years, I dressed somewhat sloppy at work, never bought any new clothes for myself, never wore any makeup, and let my hair hang straight without styling it at all. I turned into a little mouse with no social life outside of the sports activities I took part in. I let myself become secluded in a life in which I eventually became unhappy and resentful. In trying to minimize his insecurities, I had actually made my own life miserable, but I could not talk to him about my unhappiness, because I had created a pattern of holding these feelings inside so I wouldn't upset him. In that respect, I made our situation much worse than if I would have confronted him about my feelings in the beginning when there was still time to correct the situation.

Gradually, over the first seven years of our marriage, I had let most of my own self-confidence slip away. The turning point came when the company I had worked for since graduating from college went through a series of layoffs, and I ended up losing my job. The community we live in is small, and at that time, there was only one other company in town where I might have an opportunity to get a comparable job in the computer field in which I worked. I knew that if I was to have any chance at getting hired by this company, I needed to walk into that interview looking and feeling confident. So, I went out and bought a professional-looking business suit, fixed my hair, put on some makeup, and got the job.

I had not realized how much I missed actually feeling good about myself and who I was. I had not done that for so many years, and it felt great! So I began dressing nicely, fixing my hair and wearing makeup every day, which of course, caused Troy to be suspicious. He could not believe that I was doing it simply so I could feel good about myself. He thought there must be someone else I was trying to look good for. Had I simply done these very normal things for a woman to do, from the beginning of our marriage, he would have had no reason to question why I wanted to look good. I was finally reclaiming some self-confidence, but it was as if he did not want me to, which was very frustrating and hurtful. It felt like he was afraid he would lose me if I gained too much confidence. If I bought new clothes for myself, he questioned why I needed them. When I dressed nicely for work, he looked at me with a sad look on his face, his eyes and head slowly drooping downward to look at the floor. At times he looked like he was about to cry, and at other times, as if he was angry. Many times he would question why I needed to look so good to go to work, and other times he wouldn't utter a word about it. Either way, I was left to feel guilty, like I was doing something wrong, simply for dressing properly for work.

Upon starting this new job, and experiencing how revitalizing it was to look nice, and to feel good about myself again, I was bound and determined to continue to do so. I had been dying inside, letting the person I was wilt away to nothing, and it was time for me to emerge, in order to live and enjoy my life again. I had gotten to the point where I had to do this for my own mental health rather than trying to ease Troy's lack of confidence.

Over all those years, I blamed myself for his insecurities, but I learned from my counselor that typically a low level of self-esteem is developed very early in life, when for whatever reason, a person feels inadequate. They never feel like they are quite good enough, so they constantly fight to try to do better, but still never feel adequate. It is impossible for them to see themselves as doing better if they never even feel adequate. They get stuck in a quandary of inadequacies and unachievable desires and have a negative self worth. Through my counselor's help, I came to understand that I had not caused Troy's low self-esteem nor his death.

I believe another reason for Troy's suicide was a feeling of failure. He had idolized his dad. Troy knew his dad was extremely intelligent in many ways, and he spent time with him when he could, trying to learn from him. His dad died four and a half years before Troy, and as he was dying, he told Troy that of the three boys in the family who were all married at the time, Troy and I had the best chance of making our marriage work. I don't think Troy ever shared this with anyone but me, but those words meant the world to Troy who had always tried his best to please his dad. If Troy ever heard someone speak badly of his dad, he was the first one to stand up and defend him. He loved him infinitely, and would have done anything to make him happy. His dad's belief in the strength of our marriage was one way Troy had finally satisfied him, and now it was falling apart. This was the ultimate failure in Troy's eyes. He felt he had failed his dad once again.

Troy was also the oldest of five children, and many times he tried to take responsibility for things. Although nobody had told him he had to, I think he felt it was his duty to watch out for his younger brothers and sisters. He tried to be a friend to them, but also attempted to guide them away from trouble. When someone in his family got into a predicament, he would defend them, and do whatever he could to help them out of the situation. He was never the type to say, "You got yourself into this, now you need to get yourself out of it." He would be more likely to say, "What can I do to help you?" Troy had always been looking out for and taking care of everybody else, and now that he needed to take care of himself, he did not know how to do so.

Many times when someone commits suicide, they leave a note behind that may give some clues as to why they did what they did. Troy had set up the scene of his death with his wallet lying on the floor next to him. It was open to Jon and Natasha's pictures. Clearly, they were the last two people he thought about before he died. Next to the wallet, he left a note. It was definitely in his handwriting, but it was written as if he was in a hurry. Maybe because he was afraid someone would arrive and stop him from going through with it, or maybe because he was afraid he would change his mind if he didn't just get it over with. That is something we'll never know. The note simply said that he was sorry, and that he loved us all very much, especially Jon and Natasha. There was no placing of blame or explanations as to why.

After Troy committed suicide, I felt like I was the only person in the world who had ever gone through this. It was just not something I heard about every day. Since then, however, being more aware of the situation because of my own experience, I have found that it is much more prevalent than I had realized. The following statistics were taken from the article, "How Our Friends Helped After a Death to Suicide," written by Victor M. Parachin, and published in the November 1999 issue of the *Eucharistic Minister*, a monthly newsletter published by The National Catholic Reporter Publishing Company.

"Officially, more than 30,000 people a year commit suicide. However, suicide authorities believe the actual numbers are often under-reported by medical authorities in order to spare a family from social stigma. Experts believe the actual suicide death rate may be three to five times higher than officially reported. Today, there is concern that suicide rates appear to be on the increase. Consider these figures:

> ➢ The suicide rate among those 65 and older rose 9% between 1980 and 1992, after a 40-year decline.

> ➢ The suicide rate for children ages 10 through 14 has more than doubled over the past 10 years.

> ➢ Three-quarters of suicides are committed by white males.

> ➢ Women attempt suicide three times more often than men, but men kill themselves four times more often than women.

> ➢ Among college students, suicide is the second leading cause of death after accidents."

Although I wish these statistics were wrong, the fact is that suicide happens much more frequently than I had realized. So if you feel like you are the only person who has ever been through this, you are not. There are millions of people in the world who understand what you are going through because they have been through it themselves. In fact, just this year I received a story, written to me in a Christmas letter, from one of my high school friends. She wrote:

"I heard a disturbing story today about a woman I know. Last Wednesday her ex-husband killed his girlfriend and their two small children, then picked up his two teenage kids (from his first wife that I know) and killed them too. He then killed himself. My heart just aches for her. And I just got so mad that if things were so bad for him, losing his job and behind on child support, then why did he have to take his kids with him. Why couldn't he just end it for himself?? And then I thought to myself, yes, Troy did love his kids a lot! He may have been suffering, but he never hurt anyone else. He gave those kids life, forever. Only God will plan their destinies. I don't know what I could say to her or write to her. The company where she works has about 200 employees in Minneapolis, and they brought in counselors for them. I guess this story made the nightly news, but I missed it. I just wanted you to know that I thought about you and your kids today, and some people or victims affected by suicide aren't as lucky as you three. I only hope there's a special place in heaven for Troy."

I also feel very fortunate that Troy was not as selfish as the man in this story. My kids and I are very happy to be alive!

Realizing that not every suicide is the same as what I experienced, I talked with a friend whom I knew had seriously considered suicide when she was in high school. I wanted to get a different perspective on "Why?" someone would ever do this. One of the first things she told me was that she had a very low level of self-esteem. She said that even to this day she has low self-esteem, but that it was especially low when she was a teenager. The thought of this woman ever contemplating suicide or ever having a low level of self-esteem totally shocked me. My perception of her is one of someone who "has it all together." She has always come across to me as a very happy, well-adjusted wife and mother. Someone who is intelligent and well spoken, who knows what she wants, knows how to go after it, and knows what is important in life. She would have been the last person I would have thought could have ever been in this state. This just goes to show that we cannot always tell what someone may be going through or may have in their past by simply observing them. They may appear to be a happy, healthy person, but are struggling with issues we have no idea about. People sometimes conceal these issues. They might not want others to think they are weak or that they are having any problems.

When I asked for her perspective, she shared some personal details of a childhood riddled with sexual abuse from an older brother, a dominant mother and a work-focused father who wasn't home often. The sexual abuse and absent family support led her to withdraw/detach herself from others. Relationships with boys didn't last, friendships with girlfriends weren't close because she didn't want to reveal her secret, and she didn't feel she could talk to her parents.

She felt alone and confused. Putting on a confident air hid her low self-esteem from others. To stop the struggle within herself, she seriously contemplated suicide. She envisioned that the school would close for the day and her funeral would be held in the gym. Everyone in attendance would feel bad for not knowing who she really was, yet she would finally feel accepted, like someone who was loved and deserving of attention.

It would be my guess that this is a big factor in many suicides committed by young people. They do not think beyond the sensation of being the center of attention, accepted unconditionally, for that one day. Instead, they become obsessed with that sensation. I thank God that my friend did not go through with her intentions way back when she was in high school. She is an incredible woman who contributes a lot to society, and I am confident she is also an excellent wife and mother.

While writing this book, I spent time talking to Barb Wheeler, who is now retired, but who counseled people who were suicidal for many years. Although every case is different, her insights may be helpful to understand "Why?" Ms. Wheeler believes many times the death is accidental; a person who completed suicide actually wanted to be discovered but was not.

She advises that someone who is suicidal almost always has a feeling of helplessness or hopelessness. This seems to be a common theory of many who have studied suicide. Many times the person feels out of control of a situation. I think in Troy's case, and for my friend who nearly committed suicide in high school, they felt hopeless or helpless, and they had a feeling of being unable to control things that were happening in their lives.

Ms. Wheeler shared a story about a woman who was sentenced to prison for killing her husband in self-defense since he had been abusing her. Because of her guilt over what she had done, even though it was for her own protection, she attempted suicide. This woman had experienced a series of losses in her life. Even though her husband was abusing her, it was still a loss to her when he died. She had also lost normalcy in her life. Hopelessness may be caused by an accumulation of losses. Not only did she have several losses, but also intense guilt over her husband's death. Some suicide victims may have felt an incredible sense of guilt over something that caused them to kill themselves.

Suicide may be triggered from an intense fear of something. Ms. Wheeler counseled a woman whose mother had died of breast cancer. When the woman found out that she had a lump on her own breast, she killed herself because of the fear of going through what her mother had been through in her struggle with the disease. She did not even know if the tumor was malignant. During the autopsy, they found out it was benign. If she had waited to do a biopsy before killing herself, she would probably still be alive today. But she was taken over by her intense fear of breast cancer because of past experiences.

The suicide victim may be dealing with their sexual identity. Ms. Wheeler once worked with a married man who had bi-sexual tendencies, and he struggled with his guilt about it. She also dealt with a gay man who was trying to come out of the closet.

Ms. Wheeler said many times the person had problems in their lives and did not deal with them very well. They may have felt very desperate. But everyone has problems, so what is the difference between someone who commits suicide and someone who doesn't? Maybe the person who goes through with suicide doesn't use their support system as effectively. Maybe they have people offering them help, but do not know how to accept it or want to accept it. Or maybe there is not a strong support system in place with friends and family, and they do not know where to go to ask for help. Their personality in general will also make a difference in how they deal with problems in their lives. A pessimist will tend to focus on the negative things, while the optimist will focus on the positive things. Therefore, the pessimist will be more likely to feel helpless and hopeless, whereas the optimist will find hope in most situations.

Several additional reasons why people commit suicide are given by Georgia Bichekas.

o   Last desperate attempt to communicate.

o   Inadequacy/discouragement.

o   To escape pain.

o   Revenge – over significant opponent if there is one.

o   Inability to express emotions causes them to become emotionally flooded.

o   The person communicates only in violent ways.

o   No coping strategies to deal with life's pain, setbacks, etc.

o   Cannot manage stress, so it builds into depression.

Ms. Wheeler talked about a book written by James J. Kavanaugh, *There Are Men Too Gentle to Live Among Wolves*. According to the book, there may truly be people in the world today who are simply not "tough" enough to survive in the sometimes cold, cruel world we live in. Kavanaugh says those people are very dependent on relationships and interactions with people around them. If they meet someone they know on the street and say "Hi" to them, and the person does not say "Hi" back, maybe because they did not even see them, they may be totally crushed.

Ms. Wheeler spent a lot of time going to high schools to talk to kids. She worked with kids and their families in suicide prevention. One of the things she stressed to the kids was that if they felt depressed or suicidal, or if they were concerned about a friend or classmate, they needed to talk to SOMEONE! Whether that is a teacher, counselor, parent, friend, priest/minister, it does not matter, as long as they talk to someone about how they are feeling. Not only is it healthy to talk about the things that are bothering us, but whoever they talk to may be able to get them professional help to deal with their feelings properly. According to Ms. Wheeler, girls are many times more difficult to talk to about things that are bothering them. "With a boy you can rub what hurts, but with a girl you can't even find it."

She also told students if they hear someone talking about death or suicide, they should never minimize those statements. If someone makes mention of their own death, or of suicide, even in a half-joking manner, they need to be taken seriously. If they mention it numerous times, we may tend to think they are "crying wolf" or just looking for attention. But the more they mention it, the more there is an indication that there is definitely something wrong. If they are looking for attention, that is what they need from you. Ignoring them when they need attention is like telling them to go ahead and kill themselves because you do not care if they do or not. In addition to giving the friend the attention they need, I feel that you also need to tell an adult about what your friend said. You may be afraid that if you tell someone about it, the friend will be mad at you, but would you rather have the friend mad and still be here or not mad and be gone because you didn't do anything about their comments to you?

Kids should understand how important it is to be nice to everyone. Everybody needs to have friends and to feel like they belong to a group. Feeling like you do not fit in can cause an enormous feeling of loneliness, especially for adolescents who are trying so hard to fit in anyway. Sometimes kids don't include other kids simply because they are not part of their regular group. It may not be because they don't like the person, but it may make that person feel left out.

While working in suicide prevention, Ms. Wheeler used a "profile" of the person to determine if they were suicidal or not. Some of the key factors she used to help determine this were:

1. Age

2. Sex

(A 40-year-old white male with two children is the most likely category, according to statistics.)

3. Do they have a plan for the suicide?

4. If so, do they have the means to fulfill that plan? (gun, rope, pills, etc.)

5. Do they have a date planned for the suicide?

6. If so, is there any significance to the date? (wedding anniversary, someone's birthday, etc.)

7. Have they recently had any significant stresses or losses in their life?

8. Are they afraid to be alone with themselves?

"If a few of these indicators are present, there is some cause for concern, but if many or all of them are, then the person is definitely suicidal," said Ms. Wheeler. "They are not bluffing. They are very serious. There are times when saying the word *suicide* to someone is appropriate and other times when it is not. If the person talks about death, it is OK to ask them if they are considering suicide. If they say yes, they need help immediately.

"When someone is depressed, they have to make a decision as to how they will deal with their depression or their problems," Ms. Wheeler said. "One option, unfortunately, is to take themselves from this life. Once they make that decision, they develop a plan to carry out their decision. In order to do this, they must have courage and the presence of mind to be able to think it through. Many times, though, once the decision is made, the person may actually have a feeling of relief. They may feel like this is the one thing in their life they have control over. They know it is toward the end of their misery here on earth, and they may be happier than they have been in a very long time." I believe this perception of control is two-fold, however, as it is also giving up control over their life, since suicide is a permanent solution to a temporary problem.

Depression and Suicide

Depression and suicide—you can't separate the two, because most people who commit suicide are depressed. However, not ALL depressed people commit suicide. Based on supporting information given to me by Dr. Ross Pilkington, I would like to share more insights into people who are experiencing depression. These are Adlerian Psychology concepts about depression and suicide. Alfred Adler was a pioneer in the field of psychology, and Adlerians are those psychologists who agree with and support similar philosophies. The information about Adlerian Psychology was obtained by interviewing Dr. Ross Pilkington. His information was collected from the works of Alfred Adler, Rudolph Dreihuss, Georgia Bichekas and others over his 30 years in the mental health field. Dr. Pilkington is not claiming, nor am I, that any of the knowledge is originally his or mine. Rather it is the accumulation of Adlerian data from many, many years from many Adlerians in the field of mental health.

> Depression is a way to avoid life tasks, such as:
>
>   1. work
>   2. friends
>   3. love and intimacy
>   4. self

Adler would identify life tasks the patient was trying to avoid as part of assessing their needs.

> Depressed people spend a lot of time with three emotions:
>
>   1. guilt about the past
>   2. anger in the present
>   3. fear of the future

These emotions consume them and psychologically poison them. I believe Troy was experiencing all of these emotions, but the greatest

28

for him was a fear of the future. He could not envision any type of enjoyable future without having me, Jon and Natasha by his side all of the time, and yet this was about to happen since we were separating.

➤ Depressed suicidal people have an overwhelming sense of hopelessness and helplessness. They see themselves in a "no way out" trap.

➤ There may or may not be a significant rival in the life of the depressed suicidal person. This is the person they must win over at all cost. Even if it means killing themselves.

➤ Depressed people fill their heads with negative thoughts that result in the negative emotions. They focus on negatives, which causes them to be depressed. Troy was definitely a person who focused on the negative. He would intentionally not let himself believe that something good might happen, because he didn't want to "get his hopes up." That way, he felt that he would not be disappointed if it didn't happen. He would set low expectations of something so he would not be let down by the outcome.

➤ Depression is a great controlling tool. People use depression to control others. Controllers may be quick into depression. Although I do not think Troy meant to be controlling, he was. He controlled how I spent my free time by making me feel guilty if it was something he was uncomfortable with. In the last few weeks of his life, while we were discussing a separation, he took our family picture off of the wall and held his hand over himself in the picture. He said, "This is what it would be like. I would be gone." This made me feel guilty about the thought of him not being here, but I thought he was referring to him physically not living in the same house with us, not that he would be gone forever.

➤ Depression is used to gain power. As children we learn there is power in looking weak, timid, shy. Adults learn to use depression to gain power and to control others.

> Depression may also be caused by chemical imbalances or brain dysfunctions of some sort.

> Depression has been called an "adult temper tantrum" by some psychologists.

> Depressed people are totally discouraged. They need a lot of encouragement.

Bichekas, Georgia. *Depression and Suicide* workshop, 1986.

Our society generally downplays depression as a causing factor in suicide. We say a person killed himself because he was "despondent over a broken love affair," because he "got a low grade on a test" or because "she didn't get into the college of her choice." What these statements overlook is the fact that many people have similar disappointments without ending their own lives. The difference is depression. Depression saps people of the ability to recover from adverse experiences. Depression, with its sense of hopelessness and helplessness, makes all failures or missed opportunities seem monumental. These experiences feed on themselves, and produce even greater depression. But, because depressed people like to view themselves as in control of their lives, they rarely attribute these failures to anything other than their own flawed characters.

Additional Adlerian Philosophies

> Some Adlerians believe that we set an **ideal** self for ourselves and then there is the **real** self. The ideal self is all the shoulds, oughts, and musts we put on ourselves or allow people to put on us. When we cannot reach the ideal self and the real self appears instead, we can become discouraged or depressed.

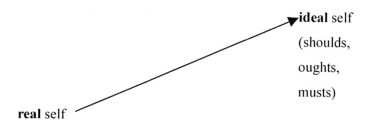

ideal self
(shoulds,
oughts,
musts)

real self

The goal is to get people to accept the **real** self as long as they are giving a 100% effort. (Dinkmeyer, Pew, and Dinkmeyer, Jr., 1979)

➢ Suicidal patients have too much personal interest vs. social interest. They focus on self but need to reach out to others. They have so much personal interest and are so emotionally flooded that they do not stop to think how their death will affect their family and others.

➢ Some people feel a need to be superior to others. Superiority leads to discouragement (and vice versa), discouragement leads to depression, depression can lead to suicide.

CareWise is an organization which provides health care advice. It is a service provided by Blue Cross and Blue Shield of Nebraska. According to CareWise, there is a large amount of scientific evidence showing a correlation between depression and harsh weather. During the winter, many people report feeling more tense, irritable, fatigued, anxious or depressed than usual. Even though there is nothing you can do about the weather, there are things you can do to combat its effects on your health.

Medications

Medication was definitely a factor in Troy's case. He was epileptic, and in order to control seizures, he took Dilantin and Phenobarbital on a daily basis. Both of these prescription drugs are depressants, but he needed to take them or he would have seizures. Troy's epilepsy was very easily controlled. As long as he did what he knew he needed to do, such as take the medications as prescribed, eat regularly, get plenty of sleep, and not drink alcohol, he wouldn't have seizures. However, if he didn't do those things, the odds of him having a seizure greatly increased. With all of the stress of the possible separation, Troy had been eating very little for the last two weeks before he died, which threw off the medication in his body. However, the weekend before he died, we discussed going to a counselor in an attempt to work out our marital problems. We decided to celebrate the possibility of another chance for our marriage by going out for supper as a family.

We took Jon and Natasha to a local restaurant, which was located in a hotel. Troy was ecstatic that we were spending this time together. There was a glimmer of hope that we might be able to reconcile and once again be the happy family he longed for us to be. Since he had not eaten in days, Troy ordered a steak. Shortly after indulging in his steak, I looked across the table at him, and noticed his blank stare at the ceiling. I tried to get his attention to see what was wrong. "Troy, are you OK?" I asked. There was no response as he continued to gaze at the same place on the ceiling. This confirmed for me that he was in the beginning stages of having a seizure.

Although his epilepsy medications had kept him from seizures during those few weeks without eating, the lack of food followed by the sudden surge of food in his body caused chaos for the medication and provoked a seizure. When someone is having an epileptic seizure, they are not conscious of what they are doing, and they are extremely strong. With a steak knife in his right hand, a fork in his left, and Jon sitting to the right of him, I was terrified that he might accidentally injure Jon or himself. I didn't know if I would be able to get the knife and fork away from him without one of us getting hurt.

Jon and Natasha had known that he had epilepsy, but neither of them had ever seen a seizure before. Their eyes were open wide while they watched intently as I tried to get control of the situation without drawing any more attention to us than there already was. Natasha looked like she wanted to cry but was too petrified to. Jon simply looked scared. They did not know what was happening. They thought he was going to die.

Luckily Troy was on the outside edge of the booth. I had been sitting across from him, so I slid in next to him and managed to get the knife and fork out of his hands. I sat beside him to make sure he would not hurt himself or anyone else. By this time, everyone in the room knew something odd was happening at our table, and every last eye was on us. The room had previously been filled with sounds of clanking dishes, silverware and coffee cups, but suddenly everyone had stopped eating. There was no longer any idle conversation at the other tables, only whispers from people talking about us. It rapidly became very quiet. Nobody was eating. Nobody was talking. Nobody was moving. Everyone was frozen and became as still and quiet as mannequins. It felt like they were all gawking at us, even though most were probably just concerned that everything would be OK. I kept my focus on Troy so I wouldn't have to look around the room to see if there was anyone in the restaurant who I knew. One gentleman came over to me, told me he was an EMT and asked if there was anything he could do to help. I was thankful for his offer, but told him that Troy was epileptic, and that I knew he would be OK in a matter of time.

The restaurant staff called the ambulance as soon as the seizure began, and although it seemed like an eternity with everyone staring at us, I'm sure in reality, it was only a matter of a few minutes before they arrived. Initially, I was upset that they called the ambulance, as this drew even more attention to us, but in the end I was exceedingly glad they were there. By the time they arrived, the seizure was over. It had been a short one in comparison to other seizures of Troy's I had witnessed previously, but it seemed like infinity to me. The EMTs were very helpful, as they offered to move Troy to a hospitality suite that the hotel staff said we could use until he was capable of leaving on his own. I don't think Troy would have been capable of walking the short distance to the room without help at this point, since he was very disoriented, confused and exhausted from the seizure. So the EMTs transformed their gurney into a chair and wheeled him to the room for me.

The hotel/restaurant did not charge us anything for our meals or for the use of the suite, which was very nice. The ambulance company did not charge us for their trip since they did not transport him anywhere, although they stayed in the suite with us until I felt comfortable for them to leave.

As we waited in the room, a gentleman came in who had recognized me from work and asked if there was anything he could do to help, which was a very nice gesture that I will never forget. I thanked him for his concern, and told him I thought we had everything under control. We would simply wait there in the suite until Troy was feeling well enough to leave, and we would go home. Then the phone in the suite rang, and it was for me! We hadn't told anyone we were going out to eat, much less where we were going, so who could possibly know that we were in the hospitality suite of this hotel? By this time, the EMTs had left. As it turned out, one of them happened to know who Troy was and where he worked, so he called Troy's employer and told him that we might need some assistance getting home. It was ironic that during the seizure I had wished nobody knew me, but now it was to my benefit that someone recognized Troy and knew who we were.

Troy slept through all of this confusion. An epileptic seizure is enormously exhausting for the victim, both physically and mentally, because of the intense, unceasing brain activity it causes. It normally took Troy several hours of falling in and out of sleep, and several times of telling him that he had a seizure before he could actually comprehend that it happened.

To sum up this story, medication was definitely a factor in Troy's case, since his epilepsy prescription drugs were both depressants. On the other hand, there are medications that can be used to keep depression under control, such as Lithium. Kay Redfield-Jamison, has written at least two books, *An Unquiet Mind*, detailing her personal experience with depression, and *Night Falls Fast: Understanding Suicide.* She has spent more than 20 years studying the origin and treatment for suicide. She also battled suicide herself. Struggling with manic-depression, Jamison was 28 years old when she took a massive overdose of lithium and nearly died. Her survival marked the beginning of a life's work to investigate mental illness and self-inflicted death.

Many times depression is caused by a chemical imbalance in a person's body, which is a physical condition, no different than heart disease or diabetes. If properly diagnosed, depression is very treatable through medication and possibly some counseling. The sad part about this is that, because of the social stigma society attaches to depression being a mental disorder, or a sign that the person is crazy, many times people who are depressed don't seek help for their depression. Many people could live happier lives and many suicides could be prevented if the depressed person would only receive the proper diagnosis and treatment. I know some people who take medication to control depression, and they are very normal, happy people. If I didn't know they were on this medication, I would never have guessed they suffered from depression.

It's Not Your Fault

Following a suicide, I think it is a natural reaction for people who were close to the victim to feel a sense of guilt. "If I had only gotten them into counseling," "If I had only said I was sorry," "Surely there must have been something I could have done to prevent this from happening," are all common thoughts to have immediately after a suicide. The length of time a person feels this guilt will vary depending on several factors, such as how close the person was to the victim, and what may have been said or done shortly before the death. What you are feeling is sometimes referred to as "Survivor Guilt," and time may be the only healer of this wound.

Keep in mind that no matter what happened prior to the suicide, there was only one person involved in the decision for this to happen and that was the victim. For whatever reason, they lost hope to the point that they could not even imagine enjoying life ever again. They saw no way out except suicide. You may have recently had a fight with the victim; they may have expressed some disappointment in you or anger toward you; you may have even known they were contemplating suicide, but the bottom line is, this was their decision. It was no accident but rather a conscious decision on the part of the victim. Even if it were directed at someone in the way of revenge, it was still their choice and nobody else's. So, no matter what happened that led up to the suicide, you cannot blame yourself.

As I mentioned earlier, Troy had threatened suicide when we began having marital problems several years earlier, but he had indicated that he could not go through with it because of our children. Therefore, I did not think he would complete the suicide. But still, I told myself for several years that I would be responsible if something happened. This was part of the reason I stayed in the marriage as long as I did.

I had a difficult time trying not to take any of the blame for what happened once it did. I kept telling myself it was not my fault, but knowing that the reason he took his life was because our marriage was ending, I still felt responsible.

A conversation I had with Troy's brother within the first few days after Troy died was one of the things that helped tremendously for me to not blame myself. My house had been filled with my family, as well as Troy's, for the first few days following his death. At one point, Troy's brother said he wanted to talk to me alone. We went upstairs to my bedroom to get away from everyone else so we could talk. I was nervous about what he was going to say to me, and why he needed to say it in private. Troy's brother and I had always been very good friends, but I was afraid maybe he would blame me for what happened. Instead, he was furious with Troy for killing himself.

We sat on the edge of the bed, and he looked me square in the eye. I was tense, and I held my breath as I waited for him to speak. Almost like a parent talking to their child, he told me, "Don't even THINK about blaming yourself for what happened." I let out a long sigh of relief and could breathe again. After hearing what he had to say, I cried, in one respect happy for his release of blame toward me, and in another, sad because I still felt somewhat responsible. I said, "I know I can't blame myself, but I still feel like it's my fault." But he wanted to make sure his point was very clear. He knew what the circumstances were, as far as our marital problems, and he had been through a divorce himself several years earlier. He told me, "I went through a divorce, and I didn't kill myself; this was HIS choice. This is NOT your fault." I was relieved that he felt this way, and I will never forget that conversation.

Another thing I feel strongly about is that no matter how bad you feel about it, or how much you would like to change what happened, you cannot. There is nothing to be gained from beating yourself up over something that cannot be reversed. It is impossible for anything positive to come out of you blaming yourself.

There are no mistakes, only lessons. We have to look at it more positively by thinking of it as a learning opportunity rather than blaming ourselves. Sure, when I look back on everything, I would like to change some things. When our marital problems began several years earlier, Troy and I discussed meeting with a counselor to help us work the problems out. We even scheduled an appointment, but ended up canceling it. We decided to try to work things out on our own. I wish we had kept that appointment. There might have still been a chance of saving the marriage, but instead, things just gradually got worse rather than better.

I wish I would have gone to see a counselor myself when I feared that he might be suicidal. Maybe they could have helped me understand how to help him. I wish I had gotten him to see a counselor. Maybe they could have helped him find hope. I wish I could have done something to help him, but I did not know what that was at the time. It is always easier to look back on life and see what you might have done different or better, but it does no good. It serves no purpose to dwell on those things. You can "should" all over yourself, but there is nothing to be gained by it. The best thing we can do for ourselves and for those around us is to learn from our experiences so that the next time we can do better.

Promises

As mentioned, much of my supporting material on depression, suicide, and grief was received from Dr. Ross Pilkington. Dr. Pilkington also reviewed my work as I wrote and gave me feedback on it. Not only does he possess a Doctorate in Education, he has taught Counseling at the University of Nebraska at Omaha for 32 years and has led Encouragement Workshops. He started conducting the Encouragement Workshops as a result of his own father committing suicide. This was his way of trying to help other people to not get to the point of suicide. It was how he reacted and dealt with his own loss, by helping other people, which is the same reason I am writing this book. In the process of providing me feedback on what I had written, Dr. Pilkington also shared some of his personal experiences with the loss of his father, and I would like to share some of his words with you now.

"I recognized my father's depression, got him to a therapist and had a contract with him that if he was going to hurt himself he promised me he would give me one last chance to talk to him before he did it. He promised. I told him to call me anytime. The night before he died he called. He was depressed. Confused. I thought he had been drinking again, but he had not been drinking. I told him I would drive to Red Oak, the town where he lived, right then if he wanted me to. I also told him I was taking my father-in-law to Red Oak the next morning, and I would be there mid-morning. I again told him if he needed me, I would leave immediately. He said tomorrow morning would be fine. I missed him by 12 minutes. I agree – it was his choice to end his life not mine. You can take the gun away from them, but they will find some rope!!!"

The lesson here is, even if you do everything you can to try to help someone who is suicidal, they may still go through with it anyway, especially if they have already made up their mind to do so. They have conviction that they are doing the right thing. They may feel that going through with the suicide gives them a sense of control and power which may, in turn, give them the determination to go through with the act.

Chapter 3

People Will Talk, and It Hurts

Dealing with the Rumors

The first few days after Troy died our house was overflowing with people coming and going all day long to express their sympathy for what happened. We live in a community of about 20,000 people, so as soon as people heard about Troy's death at church or read about it in the newspaper, many stopped by to drop off food or bags of groceries, and to tell me how sorry they were about what happened. It was heartwarming to think that so many people cared about us and offered to help with anything we needed. I remember thinking to myself how lucky we were to have so many great friends.

We were so smothered and sheltered from the rest of the world that it did not even occur to me that anyone out there would treat us any differently concerning our loss. I thought everyone would react in this same supportive manner. I could not have been more wrong. After Troy committed suicide, and we were in agony attempting to cope with it, people were circulating rumors about Troy, about myself, and about our family, only adding to the misery. As people struggled to understand why Troy committed suicide, they searched for answers to that infinite question, "Why?" In their quest for answers, many times incorrect conclusions were made.

Once the first few days had passed and Troy's funeral was over, the people who were supportive of the kids and me had to go back to their normal lives. And so did I. However, for me, "normal" wasn't the same as it had been before this happened. In fact, I didn't know what normal was any more. I had a totally new life to adjust to before I would ever know what normal was again. Going back to work, and out among people who weren't at my house to comfort me, was when I realized that not everyone would be as supportive as the people who had been there for me. After being exposed to some of the rumors that were circulating, I began to think a lot of people were cruel and uncaring, with absolutely no concern whatsoever with the well being of my kids and me. I firmly believed their sole intention was to cause even more pain and agony than what we were already going through. I became very bitter.

In the months that followed, friends tried to keep me informed as to what was being said about me and about my situation. I had not yet gone back to work when I heard the first rumor. Troy's sister, Tracy, returned to work the day after his funeral. People approached her and asked if it was true that her family hated me, blamed me for what happened, and wouldn't even speak to me. This was my first warning that stepping back into the public eye would not be easy.

Tracy and I have always been friends, and are probably even closer today than we were when Troy died. I will always remember her divulging this reality of what people thought. She stopped at my house to tell me about the things people were asking her about what happened so I would be prepared for what I would have to face when I went back to work. We sat in the family room as she shared with me the thought people had about her family hating me. After having been sheltered by the love of people who cared about me, including her family, I was shocked to hear this. My emotions rocked back and forth like I was on the deck of a ship on a stormy sea. I went from shock to laughing at the absurdity of this theory. Then I went from laughing to feeling hurt at the thought that people would say this, clearly with no knowledge of the relationship I had with the family. After feeling hurt I became angry. As I looked up at the family picture of myself, Troy, Jon and Natasha on the wall, I thought, "How can people say things like this when they obviously don't really know what they are saying?"

I have come to the conclusion, however, that the people spreading that rumor did not know me or his family, because it could not have been further from the truth. Troy's family was as supportive as they could be. From the day he died until this very day, his family has never treated Jon, Natasha, and me any differently than before he died. We are still invited to all family gatherings; we gladly attend them and enjoy spending time with Troy's family very much. I hope it will always be that way. I'm confident it will.

As I mentioned earlier, I sought counseling immediately following Troy's death. Within the first few weeks, I went to my first session. While I was there, a friend took care of Jon and Natasha for me. She worked at the same company as I did, and her husband worked with and was good friends with my brother. They worked in a different department at the same company as me.

When I returned from my counseling session, my friend told me of another rumor she had heard at work, as she thought I would want to know about it. This rumor was that I was having an affair with someone in the department which my brother and her husband worked in, and that I was planning to relocate with him due to some restructuring within the company. I didn't know anyone from that department other than my brother, and a couple of his close friends, and I didn't even know them very well.

As my friend told me this, I almost had to laugh because the only logical conclusion was that people must have assumed my brother and I were having an affair when they saw us standing in the hallway talking, or him in my office or me in his office! People had been asking my friend about it since her husband worked in the department in question, and she had been setting them straight that he was my brother.

A few nights later, my brother tried to break the news to me that this rumor had been going around, not knowing that I already knew about it. He was surprised and relieved that I was accepting it and laughing about it.

Although I laughed about it at first, since I knew how ridiculous it was, when I would tell someone about this rumor and it's absurdity, they usually had already heard the rumor themselves. The more I became aware of how widespread it had been and the more times I realized that someone else had heard the rumor, the more my feelings transitioned from laughing about it to being very angry about it. I was so vulnerable at this time in my life, and it was difficult for me to understand how people could be so cruel. I thought, "As if what I am going through is not difficult enough already, and people have to add to my pain by spreading rumors about me?" Over the years, though, I have come to the understanding that people weren't being intentionally cruel. They were simply trying to make sense of it, the same as I was. In absence of information, people tend to make up their own conclusions so that things make sense.

It's like when we are little and we open the door to a dark room. What is our immediate reaction? What do we THINK is in there... the boogeyman, or maybe a monster? We assume the worst, but we create reason for our thoughts, which are about the dark and what we cannot see. Those who could not see the rationale Troy had for taking his life may have assumed there was something terrible; a monster that drove him to it. They may have even looked at me as the "monster" and assumed or even gave reason to his rationale that I drove him to take his life, even though it was his own choice.

Three months after Troy died, stemming from a desperate need for companionship, I began dating someone who lived in a town several hours away from Columbus, where I lived. However, he was originally from Columbus. My new companion had two friends who had known Troy, and who had heard the rumors that I had been having an affair. Each of them responded in the same way when he told them he was seeing me. They both asked him, "Do you know who that is???" and "Were you the one?" They wanted to know if he was "the one" I was supposed to be moving with that had theoretically caused Troy to take his own life. I had never even met either one of these friends of his, and I was not sure if they would know who I was if they saw me, so how could they say these things about me? Finally now, years later, I can laugh at those rumors.

Judgment Through "Programming"

Recently I attended a Toastmasters meeting where there was a guest speaker, Larry Marik, who does a lot of speaking around the world, representing the banking industry. A demonstration he did for us was very enlightening. He selected an assistant from the audience and role-played. He told her to pretend she was coming into the bank and was sent to him to get help with a loan. After a brief introduction of himself to her, he asked what she thought of him and if she would want to do business with him. She said yes, she would do business with him. Then he pulled a clip-on earring out of his pocket and put it on his left ear. He introduced himself the same way he had previously, only this time with the earring dangling from his ear, and when he asked if she would want to do business with him, her reaction was much different.

She had a stereotype against men who wear earrings, because "Men shouldn't wear earrings." Even though he was the same person who was nicely dressed in a suit and tie, and he addressed her in exactly the same way, she no longer wanted anything to do with him because of the earring. This stereotype comes from our "programming" very early in life, Larry said. We buy into rules, regulations, convictions, beliefs, perceptions and values by the age of seven. Adler calls this our "private logic." For instance, if we grow up around prejudice against people with long hair or against Spanish-speaking people, we will tend to make assumptions about those people based on this "private logic," for the rest of our lives.

Once our private logic is established, we then set up a lifestyle based on it. We learn from our parents and others around us what is "normal," what is acceptable and what is not, and what to like about others. If one of our parents does something as small as making a negative comment about a person of another race, religion or gender, we usually buy into the same logic our parent used to make that comment.

We do not like it when others are "different." We are around our parents the most as a child, so we often buy into their private logic. This may backfire on us later in life. Larry's moral to this story was that "When you see something that is cosmetic, look for what is real." The earring didn't make him a different person than he was without it.

I love this story, because it is so true and happens all the time. We judge other people by their appearance, by the things they do and by the things we hear people say about them, without ever having any firsthand experiences with the person. I thought to myself, about how many times I thought I disliked someone I played volleyball or softball against, maybe just because their team beat my team. I may have never met the person, but I just knew I did not like them. Many times, when I meet the person some time later, I find out they are actually very nice. I have been guilty of basing my judgment of people on the wrong information, on assumptions I made about them rather than facts. That's when I realized that this was probably the same reason people got involved in gossiping about me. Since I knew there were times I had been guilty of unfair judgment of others, I needed to forgive others for unfair judgment of me.

I know some people who honestly do not care what anyone thinks or says about them. Maybe that's a good thing in some respects. It shields you from being hurt by other people's comments. However, it may also make you insensitive to other people's feelings. Probably somewhere in the middle is the most healthy and appropriate. We should care about what others think, but not allow it to control and consume us.

I am the type of person who cares very deeply what other people think about me so the whole rumor situation was very difficult for me. It took me a long time to get over the fact that people were talking about me. As much as I tried to tell myself that it didn't matter, it still hurt. I finally convinced myself that I should not worry about those people who were talking about me, because they were not my friends anyway. The people who were my friends, who REALLY knew me and knew what happened, were the only people I should care about what they thought.

"A real friend is one who walks in when the rest of the world walks out."

- Author unknown

When something tragic happens to you, you really do find out who your true friends are. I had several friends tell me that when people were gossiping and spreading rumors about me, they stood up and told them they knew me and that what they were saying simply was not true. That is a real friend—one who will risk making someone else mad because they oppose what they are saying, in order to stand up for their friend.

Looking back, I think my anger toward the rumor spreaders was a natural reaction, and it was OK for me to be angry for a period of time. But for my own healing, it was important for me to learn to forgive. Otherwise, I would hang on to that resentment and frustration toward those who appeared to be judging me, when in reality all they were doing was searching for answers where there were none.

The other thing I came to realize that helped me get past the rumors, was that many of the people who were talking about me did not even know who I was if I walked into the room. Yes, there were definitely those who did know who I was when they talked about me, but many of them did not. It made it easier for me to deal with by thinking most people did not even know me but were just talking to gossip. Since we live in a small town, whenever something like this happens, it is the "hot topic" of conversation at the time. People used to tell me that as soon as there was some other tragedy, I would be out of the spotlight and people would stop talking about me, and start talking about someone else. I remember thinking to myself, "That's supposed to make me feel better? I'm supposed to wish something bad on someone else so people will stop talking about me?" This theory didn't make me feel better, but it was true.

Nobody really knows why people say and do what they do. People tend to assume the worst in others rather than assuming their innocence. I was assuming the worst in people in how I reacted to the gossiping, and in a sense, they were assuming the worst about Troy and me in the things they were saying about us. None of us assumed innocence of each other. We all need to make a choice to assume the innocence of others because there may be a reason, not apparent to us, for people to behave the way they do.

After years of anger and bitterness toward people for the gossip and rumors spread about me, I finally came to some conclusions that have helped me cope with it. First of all, by letting the rumors bother me, I am only hurting myself further. If I ignore them and do not let them get to me, they cannot hurt me. Also, no matter what I do, I cannot control what people say. I can only control myself and my reactions to what they say. In retrospect, it's unfortunate that I lived with this bitterness for so long. I wish, now, that I had been able to let it go much faster, but it took understanding the nature of people to be able to let the anger go. I hope others who deal with rumors are not bound by them for nearly as long as I was.

Another thing I have come to believe is that people were not spreading rumors with the sole purpose of hurting me. I think if that were the case, they would have said those things directly to my face, rather than behind my back. I am trying to change my attitude to always look for the best in other people rather than the worst. I don't think most people really realize how much they are hurting others when they spread gossip about them. If the people who gossip were ever put in the position of being the center of the rumors, and could see firsthand how hurtful they are, they would probably stop spreading them. Maybe gossipers think those rumors don't ever get back to the person, but believe me, they do. I think friends who share these rumors with the person being talked about, do it in an effort to give the person an opportunity to defend themselves, and simply to make the person aware of what is being said. Personally, I would rather know what people are saying about me than to find out a year later and feel like I had been made a fool of.

It is human nature to want to know the details of what is happening in other people's lives, but we need to learn to direct that desire in a positive manner rather than a negative one. If we hear of something that has happened to someone, we should reach out to try to help the person, rather than spreading rumors which we usually have no proof of the validity, and which do nothing but hurt the person even more than they have already been hurt.

The Think ~ Feel ~ Act Concept

Shared by Dr. Pilkington, The Think ~ Feel ~ Act Concept helps people gain control over their emotions and behaviors. When we see, hear, smell, taste, or touch something, our brain kicks in gear, and we think immediately. What we think about what we just heard determines our emotions. We create our emotions by what we think. We are the creator of our emotions; they just don't land on our shoulders. Then we use the emotions we create by how we process what we heard, saw, and so forth, to pull off our behaviors.

Emotions are like the gas in a car. They move us forward. If we think negative thoughts, we create negative emotions, which prevents us from doing our best at a task. If we think positive thoughts, we create positive emotions, which helps us reach our peak performance. Thus, no one can MAKE us angry, sad, and so forth, unless we allow them to do so by what we CHOOSE to think about the event.

No one can push our emotional buttons unless we let them by how we process things. When someone says, "She made me mad," that is incorrect. You made yourself angry by thinking negative thoughts, which created your own anger. When an event occurs, if you have positive thoughts, it will create positive emotions, which will aid in your coping. What we think determines how we feel about something, and how we feel about it determines how we will act. So we can control how we will react to what someone says by what we think and feel. If we choose to think positively, we can consider the source and reach our peak performance.

We can also learn "thought stopping" or "competitive thought processing." In other words, we need to learn to quickly change our thoughts from negative to positive and develop positive emotions by stopping the negative thoughts and negative emotions. Recognize when you are having a negative thought or emotion and make a conscious effort to change it to a positive one. WE ARE WHAT WE THINK!!! (Corey, G., 1996)

"No one can make you feel inferior without your consent."

— Eleanor Roosevelt

One thing I have always taught Jon and Natasha is that they should think about what they are about to say about someone before they do so, and if it would hurt that person, then they should not say it. They should put themselves in the other person's shoes and think about how it would feel if someone said the same thing about them.

I have always encouraged them to be nice to everyone in their class, not just the "popular" kids. I want them to think about how it would feel to always be the one left out of the group or to be playing by themselves at recess because they had no friends. I worry about the kids who get teased a lot, and who don't have very many friends. I think about how lonely that must be for them, and I'm sure this makes them more susceptible to

45

committing suicide out of loneliness. We should accept others, and true acceptance is accepting those who are different than we are. After all, if everyone walked, talked, looked and acted like the "ideal" person we perceive, what a boring world this would be. How would you be attracted to one person over another if everyone was exactly the same? We should look for the differences in others, and respect them for those differences rather than mocking them for those differences.

For Christmas one year, I gave Jon *Chicken Soup for the Teenage Soul* and I gave Natasha *Chicken Soup for the Kid's Soul*, and they loved their books. They kept them by their beds so they could read a story or two before they went to sleep at night. One night, Jon shared with me the story he read, which was about a girl, close to his age, who had no friends and was planning to commit suicide. She had written a suicide note and went to the mailbox to leave it for her mom and dad. When she picked up the mail for that day, she noticed there was a letter for herself. It turned out to be from a boy she had met through a church group saying maybe they could become friends. She never committed suicide. All she needed was the hope that she might have a friend in this person. He saved her life.

Jon and I talked about this and I told him "That is why I always tell you to be nice to everyone. You have to realize how difficult it must be for that person who has no friends, how lonely it is. Try to understand how they feel by putting yourself in their shoes." I encourage Jon and Natasha also to include the less popular kids in their activities, in hopes that some of their friends will follow their example and be nice to them also. You just never know when you might save someone's life by being a friend to them, rather than taking part in making fun of them and excluding them.

"We are not here to see through one another, but to see one another through."

- Author Unknown

I know that I am by no means perfect. It is very easy to get caught up in a gossip session and end up being part of the spreading of rumors. And I'm sure I was worse about it prior to Troy's death, because I did not realize how hurtful it could be to those who are being talked about. However, ever since I have been the victim of the rumor mill on numerous occasions, I have tried very hard not to become a part of it. I have come to realize that many times the gossip we hear is not even true, so why spread it further? If we did not see something for ourselves, how can we make the assumption that it is true? As mentioned earlier, we need to assume innocence in others. We all have to hold ourselves accountable for what we think and feel about others, especially if those others have thoughts about us as a survivor of a suicide. Assume their innocence.

Even if a rumor we hear IS true, we do not know all of the circumstances that lead up to what happened, and I do not believe any of us have the right to judge what someone else has done. The only one who can make a judgment as to how someone has lived life, is God himself. The rest of us all need to leave that awesome job to Him. Until we have walked a mile in someone else's shoes, we really have no idea what they have been through or what may have caused them to act or react in a certain way, so **Judge not, lest we be judged!**

Chapter 4

It's OK for You to be Happy Again!
The Guilt of Going On With Life

After Troy passed away, I was shocked to learn what the company policy was for losing a spouse. I was only allowed four days away from work before I was expected to return without losing any pay. I had a hard time believing that I was to "return to normal" in less than a week's time! I was supposed to be back to work, attending meetings as usual by the following Friday. I had been sheltered from reality for this brief period of time, and the thought of going back out in public to face the world was terrifying!

I was blessed with a supervisor at the time that was very understanding when I called in to see if there was anything I could do to extend my time away from work. That first day back, he did not require that I stay the entire eight hours. He said I needed to at least make an appearance. There were days when I would simply go into his office and tell him I needed to get out of there, and he always understood. He may have gone against company policy a couple of times, but in the long run he helped my mental health so I could eventually become a productive employee again.

Since we live in a community of about 20,000 people, an event of this sort was undoubtedly heard about by most, if not all, of those 20,000 people. So I knew people in town were talking about it. And since I work for one of the largest employers in town, with roughly 650 employees in the office at that time, just walking into the building for the first time since Troy's death was probably one of the most difficult things I have ever had to do in my entire life.

That first day, I did not show up at 8:00 when I knew there would be many people arriving. I got to work at an odd time so I would not have to face anyone. Even so, walking across the parking lot seemed to take an eternity as I felt like I was moving in slow motion. And maybe I was, since I did not have the energy level I had been accustomed to. Every step I took was a major effort, as my legs and arms felt like they were each 20 pounds heavier than normal. I walked with my head down so I would not have to make eye contact in case I ran into someone. It felt as though there were eyes on me, watching me, whispering about me. I thought people were probably of the opinion that I had done something to cause Troy to do this. I also felt somewhat shameful, and that people would think those who commit suicide are crazy. I felt guilty by association, and that people would assume the entire family, including me, was crazy also.

Finally, I was safely inside. I was not totally safe, however, until I reached my office, my little piece of the world where I could hide from everything and everyone, I hoped. Luckily, my office was not far from the door to the building, so usually I could quietly sneak in without anybody seeing or stopping me. The way I was sneaking around, I felt like a burglar who had just robbed a bank but didn't get caught. For weeks, even months, I avoided entering the hallways at work at all costs. I would sneak into the bathroom if absolutely necessary, but was very glad that it was a short distance from my office and that I barely had to make an appearance in the hallway to get to it. I hung my head and was afraid to make eye contact with people. Whenever someone made conversation with me, if I smiled, I felt guilty, wondering if people thought I was actually enjoying life to some extent. I would think to myself, "Oh no, I wonder if anyone saw that," and my face would quickly turn back to stone. Although I had told myself that I couldn't be held responsible for Troy's death even though I knew it was because of our marital problems, I felt guilty, as I thought other people would think I was responsible. I wished there was something I could do to reverse this so it would never have happened, but I couldn't.

I wasn't sure how long it was supposed to last, but I knew that part of the grieving process was a period of sadness or depression. I felt guilty that I had not experienced that stage for a long enough period of time. I don't know if people really expected me to be unhappy because of what happened, or if I just perceived it to be their wish, but I thought I was supposed to be grieving. I did not feel like I had the right to be happy again. I was making my life harder by trying to live up to other people's expectations, or the expectations I thought they had. I spent several months feeling guilty if I so much as smiled, God forbid I should actually be caught laughing! All of this was very difficult for me, because I am a people person. I enjoy making eye contact with people, smiling, and saying hello or good morning, if only to see that I have made someone else smile, and I definitely enjoy laughing.

According to Dr. Pilkington, "Humor is a great coping and stress management technique. When we can laugh at ourselves, we are well on the

49

road to recovery. When we can laugh at our setbacks, we can survive them. Humor helps us cope with things we cannot change. It is therapeutic, as we can hardly laugh and cry at the same time!"

Through time, I finally got to the point that I felt it was OK for me to smile again, but it was still difficult for me to walk through the halls at work, into a local restaurant, or down the streets in town. It took me at least two years before I could meet someone in the hallway at work without thinking to myself "I wonder if they know who I am." "I wonder if they know what happened." "I wonder what they thought or said about what happened." The majority of the time, they were probably not thinking anything at all about me and had probably forgotten about what happened. They were simply saying good morning, just like they would to anyone, but I could not help thinking those thoughts every time I said hi to someone for at least two years. I don't know exactly when I stopped having those thoughts, or when it felt OK to smile again. It was a gradual healing over time.

This was nothing more than an added stress I gave to myself. Nobody had TOLD me that I should not be happy again, so I did not know that was what people wanted. Even if people did expect me to grieve forever, that was simply a selfish act on their part. We ALL deserve to be happy! We need to have hope that life will get better. Hope that there is light at the end of the tunnel rather than a train. Hoping for happiness provides healing and closure. I had hopes that my children and I would get through this loss and go on to lead happy, healthy lives.

We all need to take the time to enjoy life. Unfortunately, many times we get so wrapped up in what other people think, or in goals, achievements and accomplishments, that we forget to simply ENJOY LIFE! We need to realize that we do have choices as to how we will live our lives. We need to do things for ourselves sometimes.

"The things you do for yourself are your oxygen masks in life."

Denise Carlson, Employee Assistance Program

Recovery From Grief

Recovery from grief is the restoration of the capacity to enjoy being alive. To recover, we usually need continuous support and assistance to ease the burden of grief. I was very fortunate to receive continuous support from many family members, both Troy's and my own, and many great friends. Judy Tatelbaum in her book, *The Courage to Grieve*, notes three key areas from which we may receive help during the grieving process or during any other major life crisis:

1. Self-support – When there is a loss of someone through death, loss of a job, loss of a house or the respect of others, we lose a part of ourselves. Therefore, caring for yourself when grieving is essential. This may prove difficult as we are not usually interested in our personal welfare during a time of grieving. However, if we neglect ourselves, the recovery process is often impeded. That is why I sought counseling immediately after Troy's death. I knew that my most important job after Troy died would be helping my kids get through it. I also knew that I couldn't help them if I wasn't OK myself. I wanted to be healthy and strong in order to help my kids be healthy and strong. Listening, honoring and expressing your feelings, comforting, and being gentle and patient with yourself is necessary, and my counselor helped me do all of those things.

Of equal importance is attention to physical needs and meeting any other concerns we may have at this time. Much self-encouragement and inner strength is needed to successfully cope with the pain of loss, and only we as individuals truly know the extent of our personal pain and which persons and/or things help ease it. I talked to myself for encouragement on a regular basis. After I would have thoughts of wondering what someone thought of me or of what happened, I would remind myself that it was OK for me to smile and be happy again.

2. Environmental or social support – The more caring people and meaningful activities we have in our lives, the more helpful our support system will be in times of need. However, over-activity as a way to avoid dealing with loss is not a recommended behavior. Close friends and/or social activities can make a crucial difference in coping effectively with grief. As difficult as it may be, reaching out to others and accepting their support is vital. Some individuals may prefer to retreat and work through grief in private, but being totally alone most of the time may well be potentially harmful. Staying involved and in contact with those you care about will be a comfort and a needed source of support. Accepting help from those who cared about me and who wanted to help made a major difference for me, as well as staying involved in the sporting activities I was already involved in.

3. Spiritual belief system and philosophy of life – Spiritual belief systems are another means of potential support in time of crises. Whether personal spiritual beliefs sustain us in times of grief is an individual matter. However, many persons report faith in God as an important source of comfort and security. Our individual philosophy of life also influences how we view and cope with life's anguish and problems. The meanings we ascribe to life, to emotional pain, to loss and death are often key indicators as to how well we will survive grief and how well we are able to restore our lives after loss. Individuals who can accept loss as part of growth in life often find their personal beliefs are deeply supportive and extremely helpful in their recovery. The power of spiritual beliefs are covered in depth in Chapter 11, "Put Your Life In God's Hands: Faith Will Help You Through It."

Grief is universal. At the same time, it is also highly personal. The easing of grief is gradual. Intense feelings eventually do diminish and disappear. We are recovering when we are able to face each day as it comes, successfully balancing emotions and weaving them into the routine of daily living. For my kids and me, taking one day at a time helped us not be overwhelmed by the overall big picture of surviving the loss.

We are recovering when we are able to invest time and energy in something or someone outside ourselves. Reaching out to others is healing, gets our mind off of ourselves and brings people close to us. Social closeness provides encouragement. Encouraged people are able to cope better and are better decision makers. We are recovering when we can think about the loss without being debilitated by intense feelings. We are recovering when we can look to the future with expectation and hope.

The experience of loss and grief can enrich our lives if we allow it. For every loss or setback, we can be better, stronger people if we process it in a positive manner. We can grow from the experience and bring new meaning to life or we can withdraw into our loss, give up and never recover. The choice is ours.

Even though, deep down, I know it is OK for me to be happy again, and I am, I sometimes question whether I deserve to be happy or not. I still experience feelings of guilt over the fact that Troy died because our marriage was failing. I also feel guilty thinking that this book may make money for myself, and therefore, I may actually profit from his death. I will admit that if the book is successful and does make money, it would be a nice side benefit, but the main objective is to be able to help other people. The greatest reward would be to have someone come to me and tell me that they were having a very difficult time with their loss, and that when they read my book, it helped them tremendously.

How We Choose to Spend Our Time

My mom was fortunate enough to be able to be at home with my two brothers, my sister and me when we were growing up. She used to say she felt it was more important to spend time with us while we were growing up rather than worrying about every inch of the house being perfectly cleaned and decorated. She said some day when all of us were grown and gone, she wanted to be able to look back and be proud to say that she enjoyed spending time with us and watching us grow up. To look back and say what a neat, clean house she kept over the years would not be nearly as rewarding.

For anyone who knows me or has been to my house, they know that I live this philosophy today. Although I was never fortunate enough to be able to not work outside the home, I try to spend whatever time I can with my kids. I try to make the time we do have together quality time. Sometimes the housework suffers for it. However, now that Jon and Natasha are old enough, they help me with a lot of the household chores so that I can spend time with them and attend all of their activities. In fact, as I am writing, they are vacuuming the floors and cleaning the bathrooms! It is not always done perfectly, but how else will they learn?

The worst part about our lifestyle now, is that they are involved in so many things I cannot make it to all of their activities. Many times they are both playing in a tournament at the same time, and many times in different towns, so I cannot make it to every game they have. They always understand, though, because they know I do the best I can to be at as many of their games as possible. I do not skip a game because I have to wash my hair. They know if I miss a game, there is a very good reason for it.

As for the things you do for yourself—whatever it is that you enjoy doing—you need to keep doing it. Find out what works for you and do more of it. Do more of what is good for you. Keeping busy is an effective way to keep your mind off of your grieving and sadness, as long as you aren't "over-active" as mentioned earlier in this chapter. Keeping busy doesn't avoid the grieving and sadness, but will keep you from thinking about it 24 hours a day. Whether it is needlepoint, sporting activities, baking, or playing cards, do not stop doing the things you enjoy because of a perceived expectation that we are all supposed to "grow up," be more mature and responsible. I encourage you to never stop "playing" in life. We do not stop playing because we are old. We grow old because we stop playing. Sometimes grieving can be such an exhausting process, that it can make you feel older than you really are. It can wear you out. But continuing to do the things you enjoy will help you not feel older. Some of the most respected elderly people I know are those who have evaded Father Time and who are still very active and on the go. To quote one of the most famous respected authorities on the subject:

"Every one of you will grow old, but you don't have to BE old!"

George Burns

The First Year is the Hardest

Jon and Natasha's counselor at school told me that the first year would be the hardest. She told me that the first time we experienced each birthday, holiday, or special occasion we would normally have spent with Troy, it would be difficult. She said we would go through those days thinking about how things would have been if he were still here to celebrate the occasion with us. The second year, however, would get a little easier because we had been through it already.

54

Aside from the first few months, the most difficult time I had was the few weeks before and after the one-year anniversary of Troy's death. For three weeks prior to the anniversary, I relived every minute of every event that occurred between us the year before. This was the time when we were discussing the possibility of a separation. Troy begged me not to go through with it, and we tried to work things out so we could stay together. We even had an appointment with a counselor scheduled on the Monday after his death. Then, of course, I relived the actual day he died. All throughout the day I watched the clock and remembered what was happening the year before at that time. I relived the planning of the funeral, the night of the Rosary, the day of the funeral, the day the kids went back to school, the day I went back to work, and so forth. I was like a walking zombie for about four weeks before and after the first anniversary of his death.

The next year got easier. I did not relive every single detail. The timeframe that I was depressed was much shorter. And every year since has gotten easier to deal with. I relive fewer details each year. The details in my memory get fuzzier with each passing year. On the five-year anniversary, I was down in the dumps for a few days. Each year, I still think about the day he died and the days of the Rosary and funeral. I remember the devastating shock and sadness I experienced when it actually happened. But I am no longer totally incapacitated for four weeks like I had been the first year.

Two days after the five-year anniversary, Dr. Pilkington called to let me know that he might be a little delayed in sending me feedback on my writing for a few weeks. In my previous mailing I had shared with him that it was the five-year anniversary, so when talking on the phone he asked how I was dealing with it. I told him it had gotten much easier over the years. I no longer feel guilty about intentionally keeping myself busy to keep my mind occupied so I do not have to relive every detail of what happened. The first year I felt impelled to relive every detail. He said, "Ah, so you're getting over the survival guilt."

I did not understand it at the time I was experiencing it, but that was why I felt that I had to relive the details and why I was down on the 14th day of every month for the first year. I was feeling guilty that he was gone and I was still here. I think that is also part of the reason I chose to write a book about our experiences. I felt I needed to do something to help other people survive the loss of a loved one to suicide, and by doing so somehow I would help make Troy's death not be in vain. There would be a purpose for it, something valuable that came from it.

Each year it becomes easier to deal with the occasions. The saying, "time heals wounds" is true to some extent. Things do get easier with time.

Troy's suicide will never completely go away for us. We will deal with certain issues about it for the rest of our lives. However, it does get easier. One thing Dr. Pilkington wrote to me, "Time does help, but not time alone. It takes a lot of hard work. You must process a lot of things and you will grow psychologically and emotionally because of your hard work and your strong goal to recover. You may receive help from many, but you must process the information. You really help yourself with some input from others. It is still your choice to recover and move on with your life."

"If you want the rainbow, you gotta put up with the rain."

— Dolly Parton

I will always remember when Mrs. Stranberg told me about the first year being the hardest, thinking "Wow! A year is a long time. How will I get myself and my kids through the next whole year?" Yet still, it provided me with an end date, a light at the end of the tunnel. I knew if we could get through the first year somehow, we were going to make it, and we would be OK. The way we got through that first year was by not looking at the whole overwhelming year in front of us. We broke it down into manageable pieces by taking one day at a time, one situation at a time. When we had a crisis come up, we climbed the mountain and conquered it. Then, when the next crisis came up, somehow the mountain didn't seem as tall, or as hard to climb. Each mountain got a little easier to climb, until the mountains turned into hills, and eventually the hills turned into small bumps in the road. Before we knew it, the first year was over, and we DID survive. Now here we are several years later. We DID get through it, and it HAS gotten easier.

"It's easier to live in the past than the present, but you'll miss out on all of the fun that the present has to offer you. Even though it is less of a hassle to take the easy road, sometimes we have to move on and take the hard road through life to find happiness again."

- Author Unknown

Jon Does Not Want Me to Go Out

Since Troy and I did very little socializing while we were married, one of the phases I went through after he died was a desire to go out and do things with friends. By nature, I am a very social person, and the desire to socialize throughout the 11½ years of our marriage had been building up inside of me, much like water in a kettle on the stove nearing the boiling point. As I look back, going out was also a way for me to "escape" from everything I was experiencing. I could go and have a good time and forget about all of the stresses of suddenly being a single parent, and the difficulty of dealing with Troy's death. I could escape… at least for a while. So for the first several years I went out a lot.

I will always remember one Saturday several months after Troy died, when I had plans to go out that evening. I had made arrangements for Jon and Natasha to stay with their cousins, like they had many other times when I went out. It was summertime. We had been outside in the sun all day, and Jon was very tired. As I got ready to go, he told me that he wanted to stay home, which he obviously was too young to do unless someone stayed there with him. I said I would call to see if his cousin could come to our house to stay with them. Then he told me he wanted me to stay home, and that I could not go. It was as if he thought he was the parent in charge, and I was the child.

I was confused. I did not know how I should feel. Was I wrong for going out and leaving them behind? Was I neglecting them? Was I being selfish? I was torn between feeling guilty and yet somewhat angry that I finally had the freedom to do these things, and now, that freedom was being taken away from me again. I felt that I had the right to go out if I wanted to, yet I was leaning toward feeling guilty that I was letting my kids down and not fulfilling my responsibility as their parent.

I did not want to neglect the kids, but I also felt like I had been socially deprived for so long, that I had a need to fulfill also. I wanted to be around other adults in a non-work environment, for the sole purpose of enjoying myself. Was that too much to ask? A good, healthy belly laugh, where you laugh until the point of tears, was something I had not experienced in an extremely long time, and I longed for that kind of interaction with other adults. The new companion I was spending time with filled that void in my life very well. We would go out, have a good time, and I could forget about all of the other stresses in my life. We laughed until my stomach hurt, which was the best therapy for me at that time in my life.

My situation was different than that of a divorced couple. I had no breaks from responsibility. I had no help from anyone, at least not on a regular basis. It was just me taking care of the kids, the house, the bills, and so forth. Everything was 100% my responsibility. There was nobody to pay half of the bills, nobody to take the kids for a weekend so I could have some time to myself. I loved them with all my heart, and would have done anything for them, but I needed time for myself too. After working a full-time job, then coming home to do the cooking, cleaning, laundry, yard work, and taking care of the kids as my second full-time job, I felt like the weekends were my time to relax. I wanted something just for me. I was empty from giving of myself to their needs, to the demands of work and paying the bills, and my own need for space/freedom to let myself feel again… to be a normal, social person able to laugh at a joke, discuss the news, and be the one who is asked, "What would YOU like for supper?"

With Jon telling me I couldn't go, I felt trapped in a no-win situation. If I went out, Jon would be upset with me. If I did not go out, I would be resentful toward him for controlling what I could do.

Out of desperation, I called my mom and dad. Luckily, they happened to be home. I was in tears because I didn't know what to do. As soon as I explained the situation, Mom said, "He has to respect your need to have time to yourself. We'll be there in a half hour." They dropped everything and jumped into the car. I called Jon and Natasha's cousins to let them know that we would not need them that night.

Jon had fallen asleep by the time Mom and Dad got to our house. I sat at the kitchen table with them for at least an hour, talking about everything that had been happening. I cried so hard I sobbed, as I didn't know if I was handling things with the kids properly or not. Up until this point, I had thought I was doing a reasonably good job taking care of them and their needs. Now, all of a sudden, I found myself questioning my abilities. Was I doing Jon and Natasha justice? Was I being a good parent, or was I just thinking of my own needs? Mom and Dad reassured me that I was doing a great job with the kids. They said they were proud of us, and that they would be there for us if we needed anything.

After Mom and Dad calmed me down, I was not sure I really wanted to go out any more, but they insisted that I go. They said they would stay at the house to take care of the kids, and that I should just forget about everything and have a good time.

Mom and Dad spent the night at our house, and the next day they told me Jon had woken up and they had a talk with him about it not being fair that he try to control my behavior. When I talked to Jon, I explained to him, "You know how you like to spend time with your friends. You like to go to their houses, spend the night, and so forth. Well, it's only fair for me to have the same opportunities. I need to spend time with my friends too."

Once I explained it to him in terms that he could relate to, he understood. He has never again tried to tell me I could not go somewhere or do something with friends. In fact, when I have plans to go out, even if only to go to the YMCA for a run, both Jon and Natasha will now say, "Have a good time!" because they now know and respect my need to have time to myself.

Mom and Dad saved me that night when they came to my rescue and reassured me that I was doing OK. It was one of those forks in the road that could have easily gone one way or the other, and it took the positive path for me because of them. If they had not dropped everything and come over, I don't know how I would have handled the situation. I don't know if I would have gone out and ended up feeling guilty for having done so, or if I would have stayed home and ended up feeling angry and resentful. It could have easily sent me into depression, as the guilt would have made me feel that I needed to go back to the secluded, stay-at-home life I had lived for the 11½ years I was married.

Many times I hear of girls who get pregnant at a very young age, and get married, only to end up leaving the father and baby. I think there are stages in life that we all need to go through, and if for some reason we miss out on one of those stages, such as adolescence, eventually we want to go back and reclaim it. I believe this is what happens to these young girls who don't get a chance to grow up before they are responsible for raising a child of their own.

I also believe this is what happened to me after Troy died. Troy and I started dating midway through our senior year of high school, and although I went to college, since I had a boyfriend, I didn't date in college, nor did I do much socializing. Three months after I graduated from college, we got married. I was 20 years old and expected myself to be a responsible adult.

After Troy died, I went back to try to reclaim those years that I felt I had missed out on in my life. I even realized what was happening at the time I was going through this. I knew this was why I felt the need to go out, and I knew I should probably be staying home with Jon and Natasha instead, but between the time Troy and I dated and the time we were married, it had been 14 years of not being able to socialize. So I allowed myself to go through the "carefree" stage of early 20's that I felt I had missed out on. I thought as long as I knew why I was doing what I was doing, I would get it out of my system, and eventually things would get back to a reasonable balance of spending time at home with the kids and spending time out with friends.

Now, as I look at Jon and Natasha, and I see how fast they are growing up, I think about how soon it will be that Jon will be graduating from high school and going off to college. I almost feel guilty if I go out and leave them at home, because I want to spend every minute I can with them while I still can. I allow myself a balance between them and friends, but my allegiance is always with them. Looking back, I feel that allowing myself to go through the stage of reclaiming some of my youth that I felt I had missed out on, was essential in becoming the person I am today. It helped me get over the resentment of having lost those years so I could move on to the next stage of my life with contentment and happiness about who I am.

Sometimes we also need to open ourselves up to family and any other support systems available. It is a great source of help for us. Sometimes it is hard. We want to think we are strong enough to get ourselves through anything, and we don't want to accept help from others, but we need to let people help us. We may even need to ask for help at times. I know I could not have gotten through my experience without lots of help from family and friends, and I cannot imagine how anyone could.

As I look back on the situation, Jon's reaction to my need to go out makes perfect sense. For the nearly nine years of his life, all he had experienced was Troy and me at home nearly every night and weekend. Although I played softball, volleyball, or some other sporting event approximately one night each week, and Troy worked late one night each week, either one or both of us were home almost every night. Usually both of us were. We probably only hired a baby-sitter about twice a year so that we could go out. Now all of a sudden, I was going out on the weekends, and he did not like it or know how to deal with it. Staying home at night was what he expected of me, based on his past experiences. He probably also was feeling a sense of separation from me. He had already lost his dad, and now there was a fear of losing me also, even if temporarily. Once he related my need to spend time with friends as being the same as one of his own needs, he understood.

Am I OK?

As mentioned earlier in this chapter, one of the first things I did after Troy died was to look for a counselor to help me understand and deal with what happened. I was very lucky to have found a wonderful counselor in Karen Kelly, who helped me a great deal. We talked about my marriage and the relationship between Troy and me. We talked about the marriage failing, and my years of unhappiness. We talked about Jon and Natasha, as their coping with Troy's death was as important to me as my own. We talked about the feelings of guilt I had concerning Troy's self-esteem and the suicide itself. We talked about possible underlying reasons for his suicide. We discussed many things, until at the end of my third session with her, approximately three months after Troy's death, I felt like I was doing quite well under the circumstances. But I wanted to know how SHE thought I was doing. I wanted her professional assessment of my mental state. Was I OK? Was I going to get through this? Would I ever be "normal" again?

I had heard about the "stages" of grief being Denial, Anger and Resentment, Bargaining and Compromise, Depression and Sadness, and Acceptance. Karen and I had talked about these stages somewhat, so I asked her, "I feel like I'm doing pretty good, but where do YOU think I am in these stages of grief?" I sat on the edge of the couch in her office, feeling more like someone talking with a friend in the living room of her home than a patient being analyzed by her counselor. The sun shined through the windows on that beautiful spring afternoon, lighting up the room and making it feel warm and comfortable. I was very much at ease talking with Karen, but I clenched my hands together as I anxiously, yet nervously awaited her response. What I had hoped and expected to hear from her was that I had reached Acceptance, that I was done grieving and that everything was going to be OK again. Her answer was very different from what I hoped for, but it was one of the most enlightening things anyone has ever said to me. She said, "You've been grieving for years. You see, your grief has been over the loss of the marriage." She knew from our discussions, that the marriage, at least for me, had been failing for several years. My grief had been caused by the loss of the marriage, and also, the loss of what could have been. My fairytale dream of being married and "living happily ever after" had slowly melted away like a candle burning down to the last ounce of wax until it finally has nothing left to burn and is snuffed out.

I remember sitting in her office feeling like the lights had just been turned back on after sitting in the dark by candlelight during an electrical outage. Had I experienced Denial? Definitely! I was in denial for years that there were problems in our marriage. I did not want to believe there were any problems and I did not want anyone else to know there were either. I put on a front for my family, Troy's family, and even for Troy that everything was fine even though I was miserable inside. I was brought up with the belief that marriage is a life-long commitment, and that no matter what happens, you work things out. I thought I could tough it out and make things work. I told myself that I had made this commitment, and I was to live with my decision, regardless of whether I was happy or not. There IS no such thing as divorce! I still believe that marriage is a life-long commitment, but when I made that commitment at the young age of 20, I really did not know what life was all about yet, much less what kind of a companion I wanted to spend it with. I still love Troy to this day, but I do not believe we were meant to be together forever.

Had I experienced Anger or Resentment? Yes, for several years! I was angry over the fact that I felt trapped in a miserable life. Did anyone deserve to be miserable their entire life because they made a mistake that they could not change? I had stayed in an unhappy marriage because I did not want to hurt Jon and Natasha; I did not want to hurt Troy; I did not want to hurt my family or his family, and it was wrong in the eyes of the church. I had been unhappy for years because I had chosen to live for everyone but me! Eventually, I became angry and resentful for that fact, but this too I held inside. There were very few people who knew I was feeling this way. The fact that I had already experienced so much anger during the years I was unhappy in the marriage, even though I suppressed that anger, was probably why I felt very little anger after Troy died. I had already been through that stage of my grieving. Right after he died, people would tell me they were so mad at him for having done this to me and to the kids. I would tell them, "I'm not mad at him. I just feel sorry for him that he cheated himself out of watching his kids grow up." Until Karen enlightened me with this theory about my grieving, I felt guilty about not being angry that Troy died. I couldn't understand why I wasn't mad at him for having taken his life, or mad at God for having let it happen. Now I understood why, because I had already suffered from anger.

Had I experienced Bargaining and Compromise? Yes! Over the years, I had made numerous compromises with myself out of hope that things would get better in my marriage. Not too long after Jon was born, I remember thinking, if we would just get a new car, things would be better; I would be happier. We got the new car, but it wasn't long before that wasn't enough. When Jon was about 1½, I approached Troy about having another baby. I remember thinking that Jon needed a playmate, a little brother or sister. I also remember thinking that if Troy did not want another child, I was not sure if I could stick it out much longer. He agreed to another child, and it wasn't long before I became pregnant and Natasha was born. I thank God for her, as she is definitely a huge source of joy in my life, as is Jon. I would not give either of them up for anything in the world, but she was one more reason I could not leave. After the car and new baby were not enough to keep me happy in the marriage, I convinced Troy that we should buy a new house. He wasn't terribly thrilled with the idea, because he was perfectly happy in the house we were in, but since that was what I wanted, he agreed.

These were all compromises I made to convince myself that everything was going to be OK, and that I could stay in this situation. They all failed. They were nothing more than pacifiers that helped me survive a little longer, but none of them could provide me with the happiness I was searching for. After trying all of these things to make it work, when it still didn't, it was difficult to accept. Realizing that these compromises weren't working caused me to experience the next stage of grief.

Had I experienced Depression and Sadness? Yes! I remember "going through the motions." I walked around, almost like I was numb, not having any feeling at all. I cried inside all of the time, thinking that surely Troy would start to notice, but I guess he just got so accustomed to seeing me like that, he thought everything was fine. And everything WAS fine, as long as I was at work or spending time with my kids. I relied upon those two things for the only source of fulfillment and happiness. I poured myself into my work to fill a void in my life. I savored the adult interaction I had there. It was usually the only time I enjoyed myself enough to really laugh a good laugh. But it was difficult to listen to my friends at work talk about getting together outside of work, knowing that I wouldn't be able to join them. I had to go home, where I felt trapped in my own misery.

Had I reached Acceptance? As I look back on it today, I think I reached Acceptance of the loss of the marriage within the last few weeks of Troy's life. When I got to the point where I was ready to end the marriage, that was my Acceptance of the loss of the marriage.

Understanding that my grieving had been over the loss of the marriage helped me tremendously to comprehend and get through my anguish over Troy's death. I am eternally grateful to Karen Kelly for this enlightenment. I was very fortunate that I found a good counselor, which was a critical factor in my healing process. She helped me realize why I seemed to progress through the stages of mourning faster than I expected myself to, and why I felt "normal" again sooner than many people might have, considering what I had been through. It helped me to not feel guilty about recovering so quickly, because I recognized why I did.

"Most folks are about as happy as they make up their minds to be."

Abraham Lincoln

Although this is a very simple thought, I think it is also very profound. Many times we blame our unhappiness on things that happen around us and on things other people say or do. But ultimately, we are the only person who can decide how happy we will be based on how we react to events in our lives. If someone seems angry, bitter or negative all of the time, it is because they choose to be that way. They could just as easily choose to be happy. In the end, I did.

Chapter 5

Something Positive Out of Everything
We Have to Search For It, But It's There

When adversity enters our life, it is easy to feel sorry for ourselves and wallow in self-pity. In the case of a suicide, there may be incredible feelings of guilt and it is difficult trying to understand why our loved one took their own life. However, as Dr. Pilkington shared with regard to the death of his wife from cancer, "Life goes on; recovery is within our realm of control."

I firmly believe that all things happen for a reason. Ever since Troy committed suicide, I have said, "No matter how awful an experience seems at the time, there is always positive that comes out of everything." We may have to search long and hard for it, but there is always some benefit to be obtained, and it is worth the effort to search.

Even though it may be extremely difficult to imagine that anything constructive can come out of a tragic event in our lives, we have to believe that good will result. If a young child dies, how could a positive result ever come from that? Maybe the child's organs could be donated to another child in order to save that child's life.

Recently, when driving in my car, my car was hit by another driver who had no insurance. What could be good about that? Maybe he needed to have his driver's license revoked to get him off of the road so he would not harm anyone else. If your Mother just died of cancer, what positive could come of it? Maybe your brother and dad had not talked in years, and this helped bring them back together.

Concerning his wife's death, Dr. Pilkington reasoned that, "Her pain was ended, and thus her prayers were answered. It put life in proper perspective for family members. The family grew closer to cope with the illness and death."

It is hard to be optimistic when a death seems so pointless, like it should not have happened, such as in the case of a suicide. But we have to allow ourselves to search for the good. Many times we do not look for the positive that comes from our situation because we are too busy feeling sorry for ourselves and seeing the negative.

"When one door of happiness closes, another opens but often we look so long at the closed door that we don't see the one which has been opened for us."

Author Unknown

It comes down to a choice that we make. We can choose to never see anything good from our situation, or we can choose to be optimistic, which will help us become happy again. Many times when I look at what I am going through, if it seems like times are tough, I feel sorry for myself. But all I need to do is look around, and I can always find someone who is experiencing something more difficult than what I am. I think about parents who are watching their children die in cancer wards of hospitals, or about people living in countries of poverty, where death from simple malnutrition is an every day occurrence. It is easy to take for granted all of the blessings we have in our lives, such as food on the table and a warm roof over our heads. When I think about my life in this perspective, and what I have in comparison to what many people don't have, I realize that my life isn't so bad after all.

Today I look at my life, and feel exceedingly fortunate to have what I have; two exceptional kids which I couldn't be more proud of, wonderful family and friends, a strong faith in God, and a good job with very supportive co-workers and supervision. The way I look at it, there is no place better than here. Many times people think the grass is greener on the other side, but they usually find out it is not. We should all be happy with what we have, who we are, and where we are in life, and we will have the most fertile lawn ever grown.

The Cemetery

Going to the cemetery is never an easy thing to do. Initially when we went, it brought back many memories of the funeral and the death in general. But I wanted it to become less traumatic for us to visit. I wanted the kids to feel comfortable going there so they would not have bad memories of the cemetery. Each time we have gone, it has gotten easier.

The first few times we visited the cemetery, Jon really did not want to go. He just didn't like seeing me cry. Natasha and I still cry when we go there. I stand between Jon and Natasha with my arms around them as we spend some quiet time thinking. Then we put our hands together and say prayers for Troy.

The five-year anniversary of Troy's death was a very cold, windy day. That afternoon when Jon, Natasha and I visited the cemetery, we huddled together, shivering in our winter coats and gloves, surrounded by snow. Natasha started to cry. While tears streamed down our faces, I hugged Jon and Natasha as I gazed down at the dark gray headstone. Troy's name was on the right, his dad's, who laid to rest next to him, in the middle, and his mom's, who will some day join them there eternally, on the left. I told Jon and Natasha, "When Daddy died, I would not have thought we would have gotten through it to be doing as well as we are today. I am very proud of both of you, and I'm sure Daddy knows how well you are doing and is very proud of you, your accomplishments, and the people you are developing into." They smiled as they looked at me, and Natasha said, "I'm sure Daddy is proud of you too."

On another trip to the cemetery, this time in the spring, it was a beautiful day outside. Upon passing through the gates of the cemetery, there is a large section of grass prior to reaching the area where the headstones are located. Wild flowers grow in this grassy area, and since it was spring, there was an abundance of them. I pointed out all of the pretty wild flowers to Jon and Natasha, but Troy's grave was on the edge of the cemetery on the opposite side from where the flowers were growing, so we drove on by. We hadn't stopped to buy any flowers to leave at the grave that day, so Natasha wanted to pick some of the wild flowers to leave for Troy. I thought that was a neat idea, so we walked over to the area where the flowers were growing, and Jon and Natasha took off running, picking flowers for Troy.

It became a competition. All three of us were running around trying to find the biggest, the prettiest, and the most unique flowers we could find. After a while of this, I decided we had enough flowers to leave for Troy, so I called for the kids, but they didn't want to quit picking flowers. They would start to come, and Natasha would see another one she just had to have. Then Jon would dart off after one he had not seen previously.

Finally I got them to complete their assortment of flowers, and we walked back to put them on Troy's grave. Although they were the least expensive flowers we have ever left for him, they were the most precious ones. I'm confident Troy enjoyed watching us from above as much as we enjoyed doing it. And he would have appreciated them more because of the effort and fun that went into gathering them for him.

Although I wish there was something I could do to bring Troy back, for my kids to be able to see and spend time with their dad, there is nothing I can do to make that happen. So I have tried to make his absence as positive as I possibly can for them. We do this by talking about him and by still loving him. I think my kids and I have all become stronger people because of what we have been through. It has become a great learning experience. We know there will be difficult times in life, but that we can get through them and be OK again. I want to ensure that I make this situation as positive as I possibly can for me, for Jon and Natasha, for my family, and for Troy's family. I want to be able to help other people get through the experience of a loss of a loved one to suicide now that we have already been through it. If I can help people, that would be the ultimate reward and in my mind, the most positive thing that can result from what has happened.

"To keep a lamp burning we have to keep putting oil in it."

- Mother Theresa

If we want to have light from the lamp, we have to keep giving the lamp what it needs to stay lit. If we do not continue to put oil in the lamp, the light will go out and we will be in the dark. The same is true in our lives. If we want to have light in our lives, we must keep feeding the source for that light. We have to work hard sometimes to find the sources to feed the light, but if we do, the lamp will remain lit. At times, the light will begin to dim. Life may seem like it's just not fair; like things never go our way. We must be able to recognize when the light is dimming and give our lamp more oil to stay lit. If we do not feed the light we will go through our life on a path of darkness.

I have seen that handling Troy's death positively myself has helped Jon and Natasha do the same. People, many times, react to something the same way they see others react to it, especially if you are a very influential person in their lives, such as a parent. In a sense, they are mirrors of you. We become models for those around us, which is especially important for kids. If I chose to be bitter about what happened or to feel sorry for myself, chances are my kids would do the same. I would much rather have them be positive about what happened than go through life always feeling like somebody owed them something because of what happened to them.

"Life is a series of decisions to be made and consequences to be paid."

Old Adlerian saying

We will pay the consequence of being unhappy forever if we choose to turn everything negative. I would like to share a story from an article, "How Our Friends Helped After a Death to Suicide," written by Victor M. Parachin, and published in the November 1999, issue of the *Eucharistic Minister.*

"A friend encouraged me to turn the tragedy into something positive. When Christine's 18 year-old son died by suicide, she was devastated. After six months went by and she was still feeling numb and experiencing the knife-piercing pain of grief, Christine sought out counseling from her pastor. One of his suggestions was that Christine consider joining a support group. The only such grief group in her community was for bereaved parents. 'I went but was the only one present who had lost someone by suicide. Although I attended for nearly a year, the group never felt right for me,' she recalls. Consulting again with her pastor, he suggested she consider forming a support group specifically for survivors of a suicide death. 'With much soul searching, I decided how wonderful it would be for me to form this support group in Donald's memory. I could turn this terrible tragedy into something positive. Thank God I did. I now conduct support group meetings for survivors of suicide. Through the group we offer friendship, coping skills, understanding and support. It's been tremendously satisfying to help others deal with a suicide death.'"

Finding something positive to result from her son's suicide was how she was able to cope with and get through it. Helping others is very rewarding and satisfying, and although it may be difficult at first, it will help in your healing process. Although the positive from her situation was not immediately obvious, once she searched for it, it was there.

The father of the counselor at Jon and Natasha's school at the time of Troy's death had attempted suicide as he struggled with a terminal illness. So she could definitely relate to how we were feeling after Troy's death. She was a Godsend to us and was wonderful with the kids. After I contacted her concerning my writing of the book, she shared this story in her letter to me. "I have given your endeavor a lot of thought and am coming up short in finding the words to describe the feelings and circumstances around my dad's death. As I mentioned, he had terminal cancer and tried to hurry the process with a self-inflicted wound. Ultimately, he did not die for ten days after cutting his throat. Those ten days were a gift to my brother and me because we were able to be with him and share many feelings never revealed to each other before. It was also the first time I had heard him tell my brother that he loved him. I look back on those ten days and thank God we were able to be with him. I cringe at the thought of such unfinished business we would have been left with if the suicide had been immediately successful."

She could have chosen to find all of the negative things about the fact that her dad tried to end his life and was eventually successful. Instead, she chose to see the good things that came out of the situation.

"Choice is such a great component of life!"

- Dr. Ross Pilkington

Oprah Winfrey talks about keeping a "Gratitude Journal." As she says, "Gratitude is an attitude." You simply write down five things you are grateful for every night in your journal before going to bed. When you start it may be as simple as Mom, Dad, Grandpa, Grandma and God. But it is a habit you get into, recognizing the things in life that you are grateful for rather than being bitter about the things that do not go quite like you had hoped. This helps us focus on the good things in our lives rather than the bad things. The more we get into the habit of recognizing the good things, we will write things like "I am grateful for the 'A' my son received on his algebra test." or "I am grateful for the sun that shined so brightly and warmly today." Or, "I am grateful for the raise I received today at work." A negative person could have looked at these scenarios and said, "It's about time you got an 'A' on your algebra test." Or, "The sun hasn't shined in weeks!" Or, "It was too hot today." Or, "I deserve a bigger raise than what I got."

We simply need to get ourselves in the habit of looking for the positive things in our lives, and this is a great way to do that. We can also try performing random acts of kindness.

One of my biggest pet peeves used to be when some idiot driver pulled out in front of me. Of course, I was ALWAYS in a hurry. I never allowed myself extra time to get somewhere, so I was usually hurrying everywhere I went. When someone pulled out in front of me and slowed me down, I got really upset. I would cuss (under my breath of course if the kids were with me). I would call them names and make gestures to them, like any of this was going to do anybody any good.

Did that person know it was ME they were pulling out in front of? Were they just sitting there waiting for me to come along, and they said to themselves, "Oh, there's Barb. I'm just going to pull out in front of her to make her mad." Of course not! They either used poor judgment as to how much time they had, or they are just not very conscientious with their driving, but it was definitely not directed at me, so why did I take it so personally? Maybe if I would leave a little bit early to get somewhere and not always be in such a hurry I would not get so upset. So I have decided to try not to let this bother me so much.

Although I still consider myself a "work in progress," I have made a conscious effort not to get upset at other drivers while in my car. Just by being aware of the fact that this is a characteristic I would like to change about myself, I am doing much better. It is much less stressful driving now. I am not nearly as tense since I am not waiting to attack some other driver on the road. In fact, now I will even occasionally wave someone on to go in front of me rather than rushing to get in front of them. Occasionally, when I'm running late, I find myself falling back into the same rut of getting frustrated by other drivers, but not nearly as frequently as before. I simply remind myself that this is a personal improvement I am working on, which helps me to stop reacting negatively. I also get reminders from Natasha. She has heard me talk about it being silly to get so stressed out over another driver pulling out in front of me, so if I ever get tense, she reminds me, "Mom, it's not worth getting so upset over!"

I used to be in such a hurry that I did not even stop to let a little old lady cross the street on a cold, windy morning. "I am late for work, so she can wait for me," I thought. I have found, though, that I feel good when I commit random acts of kindness. Whether I stop to let a little old lady cross the street or smile at someone who looks sad or lonely. It feels good to see that person smile back. And what did the smile cost me? Nothing. What did it do for them? It may have been the only time they smiled that day. Not only have I done something nice for someone else, it makes ME feel good too, so everybody wins. Life is what we make it, but many times we blame others for our moods, our attitudes, and our actions. We need to take responsibility for those things ourselves.

"Pump Up Your Attitude"

After Troy died I began offering a workshop entitled "Pump Up Your Attitude." In this workshop, I discuss the fact that your attitude is your choice. You must think positively (positive self-talk) because your mind is a very powerful tool. Your mind can actually cause your body to break down if you let it.

I had a very good friend who died of cancer several years ago. He had battled with cancer for seven years. In fact, he had been battling it several years before I even met him. I firmly believe it was his positive attitude about beating the cancer that kept him alive all of those seven years. He went through chemotherapy treatments, but he always kept a healthy attitude about it. He beat the cancer and was in remission... and then it came back. I remember stopping by his office one day, and he told me that he had just spoke with his doctor and there were no signs of the cancer from his checkup... and then it came back. He fought again, never giving up, and he beat it again. No signs of the cancer... and then it came back.

This happened several times over the course of those seven years, but I never once heard him complain about the pain and suffering he was going through. I never saw him feel sorry for himself or ask, "Why did this have to happen to me?" Instead, he always had a kind word to say to everyone and always had a smile on his face. In fact, whenever I was having a bad day, I knew I could go to him, and I would get a word of encouragement and his warm smile, even though whatever it was that I was upset about wasn't nearly as difficult as what he was going through with his battle with cancer.

He was the perfect example of someone who had the right attitude about life. He was someone we could all learn from. He could have chosen to be bitter about the cards life had dealt to him, but instead he chose to be positive about it. In fact, even in the end when he was about to die, he told a family member that if he had his life to live over again, he would not want it to be any different. He would CHOOSE to go through the pain and suffering of the cancer again, because he felt it had made him a much stronger, more insightful person.

On the other hand, I know of another person who had been through several difficult situations in a short period of time. He had been through a divorce, which is never easy. He had been having disciplinary problems with his kids, and a lot of stress and pressure at work. He began developing health problems and when he started having chest pains, he went to a cardiologist to see what was wrong. As the cardiologist hooked him up to the heart monitor, they talked. Whenever they discussed the divorce, the disciplinary problems, or anything stressful to him, his heart literally started to skip a beat. When the conversation returned to every day things like the weather, it returned to a normal pace. Your mind is very powerful, and it can literally overtake your body. So if your mind can affect your body, we need to have it affect it in a positive way, rather than a negative one.

We also need to be persistent about our attitude. I have attended motivational seminars, which have made me feel great! I leave after a full day of nothing but motivational speakers, and I am on top of the world! I vow to change my ways and become a better, happier person. The next morning when I go to work and receive a phone call from an angry co-worker, it can set me right back to the way I was before the seminar. We are creatures of habit, and it takes a lot of work and a conscious effort to change behaviors we have had for a number of years, but it CAN be done! I have tried hard to be more positive, and have worked on it for a long time, but it has been well worth the effort. It feels good to think that I have made a conscious effort to change myself for the better. I think I am a better person today, but I still have a lot of work to do. We have to recognize the fact that it takes hard work every day until it becomes our nature to be positive and non-judgmental of others.

Change is not easy. People change when the price of the old behavior becomes too great. We rationalize that the old has worked for a long time, so we believe it is OK to stay the same, even if it is really not. Our motivation to change comes from the extent of the price we pay not to change. We are what we think. If we change negative thoughts to positive thoughts, we will replace negative emotions with positive emotions. It is within our control. It is a choice we make.

One thing we can do to try to be persistently positive is to hang on to the little things in life that make us happy. All of us have good things happen to us in our lives, but unfortunately, usually, we enjoy those things for the moment, and then we let them go. We need to hang on to those things that make us happy, the things that make us feel good. Then when we are having one of those bad days, or someone has upset us, we need to go back to the things in life that make us happy and focus on them. We need to do more of what works for us. Revisit happy memories, quiet places, and pleasant thoughts. We will have less time for negatives, if we do positive things. It becomes competing behaviors, since it is hard to do both at the same time.

Several years ago, shortly after I received voice mail at work, my kids gave me a precious gift that I still hang on to. I was away from my desk one day, and when I returned I noticed that I had a message on my voice mail. I was in the process of transitioning to new job responsibilities, so I was feeling very overwhelmed by all of the new things I was learning. It had been one of those tough days when I really could have used a little pick-me-up. I let out a long, heavy sigh as I sat in my chair and picked up the phone to listen to the message. I was expecting a call from someone who needed help with something, and this would just add to my long list of things to do.

I was pleasantly surprised to hear Natasha's voice on the message. She had just gotten home from school and wanted to know what time her and Jon were to baby-sit that night. She rambled a little in her sweet, fast-paced little girl's voice, and ended the message with a lower tone as she said, "Love ya, bye." Then she whistled into the phone and said, "She's pretty!" Now, obviously, she is biased since she is my daughter, but that message was a Godsend to me at a time when I needed it. It warmed my heart, put a huge smile on my face and made me feel great! Suddenly, all of my other troubles just did not seem that important any more. I must have replayed that message five times that day. Normally, I delete my messages after listening to them and acting on them, but not this one. This message has been saved ever since the first day I listened to it.

Jon obviously heard me telling Natasha how much I enjoyed her message and how good it made me feel, because the very next day he left me a voice mail message where he asked if we could play handball that night and then ended it by whistling and saying, "She's pretty!" Now, several years later, when I am having a really bad day, I go to my voice mail and play those messages back. No matter how many times I listen to them or what is happening in my life at the time, they always put a smile on my face and make me feel good. So hang on to those "little" things in life that put a smile on your face and make you feel good.

You must also have the ability to laugh at yourself. Sometimes we do stupid things, but everyone does. We have the choice to either laugh about what we have done or to be terribly embarrassed and hide the fact that it happened. Laughing about it is the much healthier solution. For a period of 3 ½ years, I taught personal computer classes for the company where I work. I will never forget one day that I was out to teach. The company I work for provides electric service to a large portion of the state of Nebraska. We service most of the rural population, so we have many offices around the state. Therefore, rather than having everyone travel to the corporate headquarters where I work, I would take the training to the outlying offices.

I had just recently started in this training position, and had previously spent most of my time at the corporate headquarters, but knew a few people from these offices from projects I had worked on previously. I was scheduled to teach a series of classes in one of our offices, several classes each week for 3 or 4 weeks. Typically, the people in the class would go somewhere to eat lunch together. The first day that I had a class, a group of us went to lunch, and on the way there, we were discussing the fact that I play softball and had been in a tournament the previous weekend.

I was explaining the fact that normally when I play co-ed softball in league, the women hit a smaller ball than the men. However, when I go to some small town tournaments, everyone hits the same size ball, the bigger of the two. The men in the vehicle got a kick out of this conversation and teased me about it a little, but I did not think much of it.

The next morning when I showed up to teach, I had forgotten all about our conversation the day before. I started up my PC, which was attached to a projector that showed the image of my monitor on a big screen for the students to be able to see. I went about my business, making sure everything was set up for the class. As students arrived, I greeted them. Since this was my first series of classes at this location, I did not know anyone in the room other than the gentleman I had ridden to lunch with the previous day. He had helped me coordinate the classes for their area, so he came to make sure everything was working OK. Evidently, he had helped me a little more than I realized. I must have stepped out of the room for a few minutes, which allowed him to do his dirty work, so I did not realize he had done anything.

I began the class the usual way, introducing myself and telling the students a little bit about myself, and then having them introduce themselves. Everything was going fine until I walked to the back of the room to turn the lights down so the students could see the screen better. As I turned around and headed back to the front of the room, in front of this entire room of people I had never met before, I saw scrolling across the screen in BIG, BOLD letters, "Barb plays with big balls!"

I thought, "Oh my gosh! What am I going to do? How am I going to explain this one to the class? I do not even know these people. What kind of person do they think I am?" I was hoping they would know this was a prank, and that I had not been the one to put that on the screen. I wondered how long I had stood up in front of them babbling about myself, as they were reading, "Barb plays with big balls!"

I simply laughed, turned numerous shades of red I am sure, and explained to them our conversation from the day before. Since they already knew the person who had pulled this prank on me, they laughed too. It actually ended up being a nice way to break the ice, and the fact that we were able to laugh together probably made everyone more comfortable. I could have chosen to get very upset with the gentleman who had done this, but the outcome was much better due to the fact that I chose to laugh about it.

When I first started offering the "Pump Up Your Attitude" workshop, I remember discussing it with a good friend. He said he thought it was great that I was doing it. Then he asked, "But do you really LIVE this stuff?" Of course, I wanted to think that I did, and I definitely believed in all of the concepts I shared in the workshop. But his question caused me to look inward and do a sincere evaluation of myself and whether or not I really did live the concepts I was preaching. The last thing I wanted to be was a hypocrite!

At the time I was a little hurt that my friend would ask me if I lived with a positive attitude. Today I am thankful to him for asking me that question. It helped me open my eyes to the fact that I was NOT always living the things I was sharing in this workshop. Every time I give this workshop and go through the material again, though, it causes me to reflect on my own attitude and behaviors. It is one thing to teach and believe in certain attitudes and behaviors, but it is sometimes difficult to personalize them and use them for ourselves. None of us are perfect, but changing our attitudes and behaviors begins with awareness. We need to be aware of when we are failing ourselves. Offering the "Pump Up Your Attitude" workshop has helped me become more aware and focus on being more like the person I want to be.

In closing this workshop, I share a poem, which I think is very powerful. If we can live by these words, we will all be healthier, happier people because of it.

"The longer I live, the more I realize the impact of attitude on life. Attitude, to me, is more important than the facts. It is more important than the past, than education, than money, than circumstances, than failures, than successes, than what other people think or

say or do. It is more important than appearance, giftedness, or skill. It will make or break a company... a church... a home. The remarkable thing is that we have a choice every day regarding the attitude we will embrace for that day. We cannot change our past... we cannot change the fact that people will act in a certain way. We cannot change the inevitable. The only thing we can do is play on the one string we have, and that is our attitude. I am convinced that life is 10% what happens to me and 90% how I react to it. And so it is with you... WE ARE IN CHARGE OF OUR ATTITUDES!"

- Charles Swindoll

Chapter 6

Kids Have a Different Perspective
Helping Your Kids Get Through It

Jon's OK!

After Troy's death, I was, of course, very concerned about how Jon and Natasha would deal with it. Natasha, who was six at the time, cried a lot at night when she went to bed. She and Troy had been very close, and she sincerely missed him a great deal. Although it hurt me to see her cry, it was almost comforting, as I felt it was a very natural and healthy reaction. She was sad that he was gone, and it was better for her to express that sadness than to hold it inside. I knew from past experiences that holding any feelings inside and not expressing them only causes them to magnify even worse than they really are. I would simply tell her I knew she missed him, and I understood because we all missed him. When I asked if she wanted me to lay down with her until she fell asleep, she always appeared relieved and quickly moved over to make room. I would hold her in my arms until she fell asleep. It was actually very therapeutic for both of us. We needed the comfort and security that came from each other's embrace, and it developed an even stronger bond between us than we already had.

Jon, on the other hand, who was eight, hardly cried at all. From the minute I told him the news, I can only remember him crying three times, each time very briefly. He cried that first morning when I told him what happened. He cried after he asked me specifically how Daddy died, and I told him he had done it to himself. And he cried one night before going to bed after I had intentionally "pulled" it out of him. I worried about Jon a lot, that he wasn't dealing with it, and that he was in denial. I worried that eventually his anger and sorrow would come out in a much more severe form than if he experienced it at the time it was happening.

Jon had overheard conversations of other people, so he knew Daddy died from a gunshot wound. He asked me a couple of days following Troy's death how Daddy got shot. Knowing that he needed to know the truth, and that if I didn't tell him, eventually he would hear it from someone else, I told him that he had done it to himself. And yet, he seemed to show little remorse. He may have actually been experiencing some anger and confusion, because he asked me, "But why would he want to leave us?" I explained to him that Daddy did not want to leave us and, in fact, that was why this had happened.

Prior to Troy's death, I had explained to the kids that Mommy and Daddy were having marital problems, and there was a possibility we might separate. Of course they did not want this to happen, but I explained to them that Mommy was no longer happy. Although, I'm sure they did not understand it totally, they wanted to see me be happy, so they accepted what I was telling them. I told them we were trying to work things out, but the possibility of a separation did exist. I'm also sure they did not really understand what a separation would mean to them, which made the situation easier to accept as well. As I explained to Jon that Daddy did not want to leave us, I told him he could not bear the thought of living life without us, and that was why when we actually separated, he could not deal with it. He could not even imagine any kind of life without being with us every day.

Jon had not been rebellious, nor was he causing any trouble or misbehaving in school. It was not as if he was apathetic, not caring about anything or not showing interest in things. He didn't even appear to be sad. In fact, what seemed to me to be very wrong was the fact that he acted so normal, almost as if nothing had happened. The fact that Jon showed little emotion about his dad's death troubled me deeply, and I tried everything I could think of to "pull" the tears out of him.

I told him I was sad that Daddy was gone, and so were a lot of other people. It was OK to miss Daddy, because all of us who knew him missed him. I told him that Daddy loved him very much and that he never intended to hurt anyone, especially him and Natasha. I tried to help Jon understand why his dad did what he did so he could learn to forgive him, but that it was still OK for him to feel angry toward him, because that would be a normal feeling for him to have under the circumstances. I told Jon if he was sad or wanted to cry, it was OK to, and that I was always there if he ever needed someone to talk to. I said he could talk to me about anything, but if he was not comfortable talking to me about something that was bothering him, he needed to talk to somebody. Whether he confided in a friend, the counselor at school, or my brother, it did not matter as long as he talked to someone if something was bothering him. All of my attempts were fruitless, however, as I still could not get him to express his emotions.

Months went by, and still he seemed to show little remorse. However, he seemed to show no signs of problems either. He had not been rebellious in any way, had not given me any disciplinary problems, and his teachers and counselor at school indicated that he seemed to be doing fine. I asked at parent/teacher conferences if they saw any changes in him or had any problems with him, and always, the answer was, "No, he seems to be doing quite well."

With all indications that he was doing great, I still could not believe it. I was sure he must have been repressing feelings of anger and sadness. I asked Jon's counselor at school how to work with him to deal with his repression of feelings. I asked the counselor I was seeing for myself how to work with him. They both indicated that as long as Jon was not showing any signs of problems, I needed to wait until there were signs. They said when he was ready to discuss how he felt about his dad's death, he would come to me or let me know somehow, but until then, I should not push the issue. For a year, I stewed over this, and anxiously waited for the day when he would finally open up, until I finally gave in to waiting until he would come to me.

My concerns about Jon keeping his feelings bottled up inside, were intensified by a statement made to me almost immediately after Troy's death. While at school one day within the first week after Troy's death, one of the teachers stopped me to ask how the kids and I were doing. When I told her they were doing surprisingly well, and that it almost scared me, she said it might be years before they really understood what happened since they were so young at the time.

That thought remained in the back of my mind and had been haunting me ever since, especially since they seemed to be doing so well. I kept expecting that some day, they would fall apart, rebel terribly, and go astray. I watched for signs of trouble and always reacted immediately if there were any signs, no matter how small. I was afraid I would lose control, and they would become drug addicts or gang members, especially without a male role model in the house. The only sign I remember was one time shortly after Troy died, Jon's teacher called to let me know he had made an inappropriate comment in class. It wasn't anything the teacher would normally have called about, but since I had asked her to pay extra attention to his behavior, she called because it was out of the ordinary for him. I had a talk with him about his comment, and we have not had another incident like it again.

My greatest fear lay in the similarity I began to see between Jon's behavior and that of his father. Whether it was his frustrations at work or his anxiety over our decaying relationship, Troy would not open up to anyone about what was bothering him. Instead, a sullen shadow would cast from Troy's face if I asked him what was wrong. His chin would drop to his chest, his eyes in a blank stare at the floor as if he had just lost the most important football game of his high school career whenever I mentioned my job or meeting someone new at work. He would swallow hard, as if choking back tears, which never came.

Like a ghostly reflection, at times that same sullen shadow darkened when I tried to have conversations with Jon about his feelings. But what was even more disheartening was the fact that many times he showed no emotion at all, like he didn't even care that his dad was gone. I begged him to open up to me, "Please, Jon, tell me what you're thinking. Scream at me, throw a tantrum, whatever!" But he would simply drop his chin to his chest, eyes in a blank stare, and would swallow hard, just like Troy did. Then his big brown eyes would slowly come back up to meet mine. They were so sad, almost as if he thought I was mad at him for not crying, but he almost never did cry. Then I would tell him it was OK as long as he wasn't holding anything inside of him. I was sure that one of those times he would finally open up and cry, but it never happened.

Finally, after 3½ years of waiting, I got my relief. Jon's sixth grade class had earned a trip to Washington, D.C., to a National Energy Education Development convention for their efforts to learn about energy and the environment. On that trip was another boy from Jon's class at school who had lost his older brother in an accident. As Jon and I made our two-hour car ride home from the airport, we discussed the relationship between this boy and his mother. Since she had lost a son, the mother watched very closely over the son who remained, determined that she would not lose another son. The relationship between Jon and me was different than this, because I had not lost a child, but rather my husband. At the end of the conversation, Jon looked at me and said, "You know, I never really cried very much when Daddy died." My eyes opened wide and ears perked up as I held my breath and waited to hear what he would say next. I tried to hide my anxiousness in the darkness of our car. I clenched the steering wheel tightly as he said, "I don't think I fully understood what happened. I think I really thought he was coming back. I think if it were to happen today, I would cry a lot more."

What a relief! Actually, relief doesn't even begin to sum up how I felt! Although I had waited more than three years to hear those words, the release from my fears of his stifling of his feelings seemed much longer than that in

81

coming. I felt almost weightless as my body tingled all over for a few seconds. Not only was it a relief to finally feel that he was OK, but it was also a relief to think that he understood why he was OK. I began to cry as I told Jon how wonderful it was to hear him say that. "You ARE OK!" I said, as I explained how worried I had been about the way he was dealing with his dad's death. I have not worried about it since, and he has not given me any reason to.

Even though I believe it is important for kids to have positive male and female role models in their lives, I don't believe that people can blame the downfall of today's youth and today's society on the fact that so many more kids are being raised in a single parent family. I think that is a copout and an excuse used by many single parents that their kids run the streets and get into trouble because they do not have a father figure in the home. Although I had a lot of help with my kids from a lot of people, great kids CAN be raised in a single parent home; so, please do not use that as an excuse to let your kids go astray.

My counselor had told me that everyone grieves differently, but Jon showed me firsthand. We need to respect that fact, and allow people to grieve on their own time schedules. Although there are stages in grieving that each of us may or may not experience, and at varying degrees, we do not grieve on any set schedule. It is important to watch for signs that there may be problems lurking within, but parents or guardians should not assume that there are!

If a child shows no reaction at all, adults have a tendency to assume there is something wrong with them. That is exactly what I did with Jon. Maybe kids accept loss better than adults, and it is not denial at all. However, it could be denial, so if the child shows no reaction, it is best to simply tell them "I will be here whenever you want to talk about it." This was a lesson learned for me.

Children and Grief

Children go through the same process of grieving as adults do, but there are some differences in the way they experience grief. I received the following information on Children and Grief from the Methodist Employee Assistance Program, and have reprinted it with their permission. For children, grief is an emotion expressed from the loss of someone or something depended upon for support, security or sustenance, which may be different than the "stages" of grief an adult would normally experience. Parents may have a tough time helping children grieve if they are grieving the same loss. Grievers may be so consumed by their own grief that they have difficulty expressing love, thus they cannot love the child and grieve at the same time.

A child's process of major phases of grief will probably be different than an adult's. Their phases of grief may be 1) Protest, 2) Despair, and 3) Reorganization. Magical thinking can cause problems for children. If they recently had a disagreement with the person who died and they told them "I wish you were dead," and then that person died, they feel guilty. They think they are the reason why the person died, because they "wished" them dead.

A child's developmental understanding of death and coping with death will differ based on their age at the time of the death, and may be something like this.

Birth to Age 4 – Recognizes death as separation. Coping method is crying or fussing.

Ages 5-6 – Sees death as a cessation of movement associated with punishment. Believes you can "wish" someone dead. Coping method can be protest or withdrawal.

Ages 7-9 – Often will see death as a final state. They still believe the dead can see and hear. They begin to look at their own death. Coping method is controlling behavior and physical activity. They may dream a lot as death is seen as a person or monster.

Ages 10-12 – Death is accepted as universal, irreversible, and inevitable. Coping method is verbal sharing with peers.

Ages 12-18 – Has all of the earlier age concepts, and has added the concept that death takes away a very caring relationship. Coping method is conformity withdrawal.

These coping characteristics were taken from *The Child and Death* written by Olle J. Sahler in 1978. Keep in mind that this is merely a guideline to help you understand how a child may be feeling, but is not an exact science. For example, Natasha was six years old when Troy died, and she is very mature for her age, but her reaction was more like what is described for Birth to Age 4. She simply missed her daddy very much (separation), and therefore, she cried a lot. Jon, on the other hand, was eight years old when Troy died, and in the sense that he tried to use some controlling behavior, he reacted within the description for Ages 7-9.

In some respects, children have an advantage over adults because they will talk and dump their feelings more than adults. As suggested by the Methodist Employee Assistance Program, DO NOT present children a lot of myths and fairy tales about death.

> ➤ "Mommy is on a long trip." The child will wonder "Why didn't she take me with her?" This can make them feel abandoned or left behind.

> ➤ "God took Daddy" may cause the "Dumb God syndrome," with anger toward God.

> ➤ "She was so sick," associates all sickness with death.

> ➤ "God took Daddy because he was a good person," says if good people die, then I must be bad.

> ➤ "He is asleep forever," may cause insomnia, as the child may become afraid to go to sleep.

> ➤ "Old people die" will make them afraid of growing old.

So what IS the proper way to talk to a child about the death of someone they loved? Again, according to the Methodist Employee Assistance Program, you may tell them that all of the parts did not work any more. They can relate this to a toy they have that is broken and they cannot play with any more. Tell them about the death in familiar surroundings. Let them know they will be loved and taken care of even though Daddy/Mommy/Grandma is gone. They need security amidst the turmoil and change.

To help children cope with their grief, be honest with them about what happened, use correct terminology, assure them they did not cause the problem, recognize the loss to them, provide a vehicle for them to express their grief, set guidelines for them and let them know they will not always feel this bad.

No matter what happens, do not hide your grief from children. They need to see you grieve so they can see that it is a normal process for us to go through so we can feel better again. The philosophy of past generations was to be strong, be tough, and not cry. Fortunately, we have learned that this was the wrong philosophy. Letting your emotions show and getting it out of your system is a much healthier approach. I never tried to hide my feelings from my children. If I was down and felt the need to cry, I cried. After all of the times I told them it was OK for them to cry, that they needed to tell someone if something was bothering them, and asking them what was wrong, now they won't let me off the hook if they see that I am upset about something. They will ask me what is wrong, and will not accept the answer, "Nothing." They will say, "It's OK Mom; you can tell me." In addition to not hiding our grief from children, they need to know they are loved, which will provide security for them.

Explain what will happen. You will feel bad for a period of time, lonely, sad and confused, but it will not last forever. I always let Jon and Natasha know it was OK to feel bad and to cry because it was part of getting over the loss. Include children at funerals. It is part of grieving and finality. When they are not included they feel left out and abandoned. They may end up regretting that they did not go, and there is nothing you can do to give that experience back to them. On the other hand, if the child decides not to attend, do not force them. If they decide to go, prepare them for it ahead of time. Give them details in advance that there will be a lot of crying and sadness, but that is OK. Tell them Daddy will be in a casket and will not look like he always did. I told Jon and Natasha that Daddy would look like himself in some respects, but not like himself in others. He would look different.

In the case of a suicide, depending on the age of the children, it may be better to tell them the details of what happened at a later time when they are old enough to understand it. However, they need to know the truth at some point. You may be able to tell them Daddy stopped his own parts from working. If they ask why, telling them "I don't know" is a valid answer, because you may not understand why yourself yet.

My counselor, Karen Kelly, as well as Jon and Natasha's counselor at school told me that I should wait to tell them the details of what happened until they asked the questions. They said when the kids were ready to hear the answers, they would ask the questions, and until then, not to push the answers on them. So that is what I did. I waited for Jon and Natasha to approach me with questions about how their dad died.

This scared me somewhat, as I waited for the day when someone would say something hurtful about it to them. Kids can be very blunt, and many times do not use much tact in how they say something. When the time came for Jon and Natasha to know the truth, I wanted it to come from me rather than in an uncomfortable situation around a group of friends or peers.

Since Jon was older, he asked the question first. It was only a matter of a couple of days after Troy died. It was probably the first time he had an opportunity to talk to me alone since our house was full of people those first few days. On the morning of the day after the funeral, I remember coming down the stairs and into the kitchen where he was standing, almost as if he were waiting for me. He asked me what happened, how his dad died. I felt as though he had been waiting to ask me this for a while, but there had been so many people around, and he had been occupied with his cousins, so he had not had a chance. He must have overheard someone talking, or one of his cousins may have said something about his death being due to suicide, but he needed to hear it from me to confirm that it was true. This was one of the very few times I ever remember Jon crying.

Natasha was much slower in asking the question about what happened. Surprisingly, we got through the rest of the school year without any episodes. In fact, she probably would not have asked when she did if it were not for an incident that occurred when she went to a dance rehearsal that following summer.

It had been nearly six months since Troy died, and we seemed to be doing quite well. I dropped Natasha off at the town square for dance rehearsal for an outdoor performance later that week. Jon had a baseball game that night, also; so, I dropped him off at the field for pre-game practice, and later, picked Natasha up from her rehearsal. The area where the dance performance was to be held is quite shaded, with huge old trees lining the street and sidewalks. I remember the breeze blowing through the trees, even though the sun was shining brightly and the temperature was warm. It was a beautiful evening, and I was in a good mood. I was excited to get to Jon's baseball game and see him play.

As Natasha and I hurried back to the car to get to Jon's game, she asked me, "Mommy, did Daddy shoot himself?" My good mood was suddenly deflated. I felt flush as my heart skipped a beat. Even though it was hot out, her question gave me goose bumps all over. I was absolutely shocked! Although we had not forgotten about Troy, we had not talked about his death recently either. This came totally without warning. In my mind, I knew I needed to answer this question for her, but it was just not the right time. We were on our way to Jon's baseball game, and I did not want either of us to be crying when we arrived. Nor did I want to miss the game. So, I put her question off, planning to answer it for her later. But by the time the game got over, she seemed to have forgotten about it, so it was easier for me to just pretend she never asked.

Several days later, I was in the bathroom, and Natasha came in and simply stated, "Mommy, Daddy's not stupid." Again, I was surprised, but this time I had a little better opportunity to question her about this to find out what was triggering these questions and statements. I looked at her very seriously and said, "Of course, Daddy is not stupid. Why would you even think something like that?" That is when she told me that a little girl had walked up to her at the dance rehearsal in front of several of her friends and told her that her daddy was stupid because he shot himself. She did not know how to respond, as she was only 6 years old, and she did not even know how he died because she had not asked me the question yet. Or if she did have an idea what happened, she was in denial, not wanting to believe it. I had envisioned that eventually she would come to me and ask what happened. It was very unfortunate that she had to learn the truth from another child whose parents obviously did not handle the situation very well with her. It had to be very painful to hear this from someone she barely knew, especially in front of her friends. She was embarrassed, so she told the girl that she was wrong.

We had been so fortunate that neither Jon nor Natasha had experienced a negative situation like this until then, that it had not occurred to me it could still happen. I thought we were beyond that point. The school they went to handled the situation so well that we never had an incident at school where either of them came home indicating someone said something hurtful. It was as if God gave us their counselor as an angel to help us through this, because she left the following year to be in a school closer to where she lived.

The rest of the school's staff was also very supportive. On the day after the funeral, following a visit with the school counselor in the morning, the kids returned to school after lunch. They only missed 2 ½ days of school. The principal's response when I called to let him know they would be coming back was, "That's great. The kids really miss them!" All in all, the school was wonderful. They took a huge burden off of my shoulders in that I knew they were being well cared for even when I was not there to watch over them.

Even though they were being very well taken care of at school, I knew there would be difficult times we would simply have to deal with. One day, approximately a year after Troy died, I returned to work from lunch and received a phone call from Natasha. I could tell immediately that something was very wrong, and I can still remember her tremulous, hushed voice. The kids happened to be out of school that afternoon, and while looking through a pile of papers on the kitchen counter, she found a copy of the note Troy had left before he died. When I asked her what was wrong, she said, "I found Daddy's letter. He really did love us, didn't he?" At first I thought she was talking about one of the letters he had written to me during the times when we were struggling and discussing a separation. Then she read the letter to me, "I'm sorry. I love you all very much, especially Jon and Natasha." I had originally put the letter in a safe deposit box at the bank so that some day I could show Jon and Natasha that Daddy's last words were that he loved them very much, but I had taken it back out in order to show it to my counselor to see if there were any additional insights she would have from the letter. I thought I had put it back in the safe deposit box, but obviously I had not.

Unable to bear the agony I felt for her in finding the letter, I interrupted, "I'll be home in a few minutes." I imagined her at the table with the letter tightly clenched in her delicate little hand, tears rolling down her cheeks. I wanted only to pull her onto my lap and console her. She said, "That's OK. You don't have to come home. You can stay at work." I told her, "I am definitely coming home, and I will stay there as long as you need me to." Even though she had told me I did not need to come home, I could hear the comfort in her voice when I told her I was going to. I left work and arrived home within ten minutes. I found her in my bed, crying and holding the letter. I hugged her and cried with her, as I reminded her that Daddy loved us very much. We talked about what happened, and when I was comfortable that she was OK, I went back to work.

Ever since their dad committed suicide, I have been very concerned that Jon and Natasha will grow up thinking that suicide is a valid solution to a problem. Since suicide was Troy's way out when life did not go the way he wanted it to, it is almost like he gave them permission to do the same themselves. Kids, many times, do as we do, not as we say. Our actions speak louder than words. I have had several discussions with Jon and Natasha about the fact that although Daddy was a very good person, he made a very bad decision, and that suicide should not be the solution to a problem. I think they understand that suicide is never the solution. They are doing great. They survived through strength and guidance from many caring family members, friends, teachers and other positive influences in their lives.

Don't Pressure Yourself to Always Be Perfect

On the same trip to Washington, D.C, that I discussed earlier in this chapter Jon and I had a terrible experience just getting to the airport. There would be 22 students and 25 adults going on this trip, and our flight was to leave at 6:50 a.m. out of Omaha. Since it is nearly a two-hour drive to the airport for us, I had hoped to stay in Omaha the night before so we would not have to get up so early, but with everything I needed to get done at work before we left, that did not happen. In fact, I ended up mowing the lawn that evening, then going back to work until 11 p.m., and being up until midnight finishing a load of laundry so we would have the necessary clothing for the trip. I set my alarm for 3 a.m. in hopes of being on the road no later than 4 a.m., but the alarm clock I had at that time did not have a snooze button on it. After only a few short hours of sleep, you can imagine what happened next.

I was suddenly awakened by a panicked, "Mom!" When I BOLTED up to see what time it was, the clock read 5 a.m. I had overslept two hours!! I immediately began to shake uncontrollably as I threw my clothes on, and the last minute items into the suitcase. We were on the road in 15 minutes, and the race was on.

As I sped out of town, crying like a 2-year-old, I looked down at the gas gauge. Of course, I had not been smart enough to get gas the night before either! At 5:15 a.m., not many gas stations are even open, as was the case with the first one that I passed. We made it as far as the next town and found an open gas station. I inserted the nozzle, and started pumping the gas. I then ran inside to pay the bill. I paced the floor until she finally told me she could not ring it up until I put the nozzle back on the pump. I ran back outside, put the nozzle on the pump and ran back inside. I gave her my credit card, but obviously, MasterCard was not awake yet! It seemed like FOREVER to get my purchase approved. I could have written a check faster.

After my credit card was FINALLY approved, we resumed the race. I was still crying and shaking uncontrollably. This would be the first time Jon would ever fly in an airplane, and it was a trip with numerous friends and classmates. He had worked hard all year to earn the right to go on this trip. It would be an experience he would never forget... especially now. How could I let him down like this!!!

I remember thinking to myself that I am the only parent he has now, and that if he cannot count on me to be responsible enough to get him to the airport on time for his first experience on an airplane, with 22 friends from his class, who could he count on? I beat myself up all the way to the airport, thinking, "What an idiot, I can't believe you did this." I wanted to do everything in my power to get him there to join his friends on this flight. I could tell by the look of concern on Jon's face and the way he tensed up the entire time, that he was scared to death at the way I was driving. He would have preferred that we drive normal and miss the flight, rather than risk having an accident.

He should have been the one who was terribly upset over what was happening since this trip was for him, but instead he calmed ME down. He said, "Mom, it's OK if we miss the plane. We can take a later flight. There are no events scheduled until tomorrow, so it doesn't matter what time we get there as long as we get there sometime today."

Although he got me to stop shaking uncontrollably, I still felt that I had to do EVERYTHING in my power to get to the plane on time so he could be with his classmates the entire trip and not miss out on any events. He had earned this trip, and I wanted him to be able to make the most of it. At speeds as high as 85-95 mph, I felt like an Indy 500 driver! I dodged in and out of traffic like Jeff Gordon. I kept crying, "We're never going to make it!"

When I heard sirens behind me, I thought we were doomed. In my rearview mirror, I watched a police car approach, but much to my surprise, it went on past me. Then there were more sirens, and a fire truck passed also. Chills went down my spine as we passed the accident with two vehicles in the ditch and another ambulance on the way. Although neither of us said anything, Jon and I both realized that it could have easily been us in that ditch. That slowed me down briefly, but not for long, as I quickly became focused again on getting to the plane on time. Maybe it was my competitive nature that told me to never give up.

As we continued our race, I remembered from the week before when I flew out of the same airport, that the highway I normally take to the airport was under construction. The only other way I knew for sure how to get to the airport was to drive through the heart of Omaha. Now I was SURE we would not make it in time. But, I thought, it's 6:15 a.m., surely there can't be that much traffic at this hour. Boy, was I wrong! It may have been light traffic for Omaha, but it was like rush hour in the town I'm from! Again, I weaved in and out of traffic, PRAYING that I would not get pulled over by a policeman, or that if I did, he would understand my dilemma and give me an escort!

As I pulled into the parking garage at the airport, it was 6:35... our plane would take off in 15 minutes. Again, remembering my experience at the airport one week earlier, I had to go all the way to the top floor of the parking garage to find a parking space. We would never make it if that happened. Someone obviously watched over us the entire trip just to get us there safely, and then we even found a parking space on the first floor almost immediately upon entering the garage.

Jon and I jumped out of the car, and divvied up the bags. Heavily loaded down, we ran into the terminal and down the escalator, huffing and puffing, to the check-in counter. As I ran ahead of Jon, I kept yelling back, "Just follow me... keep going, you can do it!"

Have you ever had one of those dreams where you are running as fast as you can from the villain, but you are just not going anywhere?? Well, that is what it felt like. When I arrived at the check-in counter, and asked about our flight, the representative looked somewhat confused. I was out of breath and shaking from the adrenalin of the rush to make the plane. Impatiently, I rocked back and forth while we waited as she checked on our flight. She then told us that our flight was a Midwest Express flight, which of course, is whose counter I thought we were at, but they were right next door. Luckily, there was nobody waiting in line at the Midwest Express counter, because if there had been, we would never make it. There were two representatives standing there in their navy blue uniforms talking to each other. When I asked about our flight, one of them simply said, "Gate 2 upstairs, just take your bags with you. I'll call from here to let them know you're coming." I breathed a momentary sigh of relief, as this told me the plane had not taken off yet. Jon had caught up to me by now, so we ran back up the escalator, through security, and over to Gate 2, where it was as quiet as a morgue. There weren't very many people in the airport in general at this hour of the morning. Everyone had already boarded the plane, and there were three people in the waiting area by Gate 2. Two people who were there to see off one of Jon's classmates, and the Midwest Express representative were the only people in the area. But I could see that the plane had not yet begun taxiing. "YES! We made it!"

I went straight to the door, but it was locked! I ran over to the attendant, PLEADING with him to let us on. "You don't understand," I cried. "There are 45 people on that plane from my son's class and they're taking a school trip to Washington, D.C.! The plane is RIGHT THERE, it hasn't even taken off yet, how can you tell me we can't get on?"

With a disgusted look on his face, he went to the check-in counter to use the phone. When he hung up, he went over to the locked door to the walkway of the plane and unlocked it! I wanted to throw my arms around him, but I could see that he was not in the mood. So, with happy tears, I thanked him numerous times. In a condescending voice, he said, "We DON'T normally do this. You NEED to be on time." As we stepped onto the plane, still out of breath, there were cheers from the crowd that we had made it. The students, parents and teachers knew we were not on the plane, but there was nothing they could do to hold it for us. We handed our bags to the flight attendants, and eagerly hurried to our seats. After tensing every muscle in my body for the last hour and a half, all of the tension dissipated as I dropped into my seat, looked over at Jon, and said, "We made it!" As I took a deep breath and let out a long sigh of relief, I closed my eyes and said a prayer, thanking Troy for watching over us... for being our guardian angel.

We made it, all right, but what had I done? Once I had a chance to slow down and think about what happened, I felt guilty about it. The entire time in Washington, D.C., I thought about it, and when I think back on it now, I still feel guilty. I had put both of our lives in danger just to get to the plane on time. At the speeds I was driving, if we had an accident, surely the outcome would not have been good. So why did I risk our lives for this?

Jon and I have discussed this trip since then and agree that I should have just admitted that I made a mistake. I overslept, but there was nothing I could do about it after it happened, so there was no point in making the mistake worse than it was by adding another mistake to it. I have told Jon that if he is ever in a similar situation, I do not want him to do what I did. I had not set a very good example for him. Why did I think it was OK for me to do something I would not want him to do? It was as if I thought I was above him, and that it was OK for me, but not for him. I have learned, not only through this experience, but through other events as well, that I need to think more about the example I set before I make a decision about how I will act. Jon and Natasha also keep me in line by letting me know when I do something they know they would be in trouble for doing. This makes me reflect on my behavior and the example I set for them.

Jon and I agreed that neither of us ever wants to go through an experience like our trip to the airport again. As a single parent of two children who do not have a dad they can call when they miss him, or to ask advice from, sometimes I put too much pressure on myself to always be perfect and never make a mistake. But I have to step back and let myself be human. I have to be able to admit when I've made a mistake and accept it. Our kids do not expect as much from us as we expect from ourselves at times, so we need to lighten up on ourselves. Perfectionism is a faulty life goal. No one on earth is perfect, but many times we try to reach that unobtainable goal.

Encouragement, not criticism

When Jon was in sixth grade, I attended his parent/teacher conference for the first quarter. His teacher told me she thought Jon was exceptionally bright. I was shocked, as none of his other teachers to that point had told me that. Jon had always been what I considered an above average student, but not outstanding. She said she had never seen a kid who could accomplish so much in so little time and get so much of it right. She said his problem was that his mind was on the playground. Jon loves sports, and therefore would hurry through his work so he could get outside for recess.

After hearing this, I had a talk with Jon. I told him that I thought if he would just slow down a little bit and double check his work, he could easily be a straight "A" student. I also told him that if he thought he would like to receive a college scholarship to play baseball somewhere, he would have a lot better chance of getting one if his grades were good in addition to his baseball abilities.

That sixth grade teacher inspired him and encouraged him throughout the year. He worked hard and accomplished a lot that year. When he took his Iowa Test of Basic Skills, which ranks kids their age with others in the nation on their knowledge in all school subjects, Jon's composite score of all subjects combined ranked him in the 97th percentile in the nation. His math score was in the 99th percentile! These scores qualified him to take his choice between the SAT or ACT college entrance exam when he was only in the seventh grade. When his SAT test scores arrived, he had scored higher in math than 56% of everyone who took the test (mostly high school juniors and seniors). He scored high enough to receive Nebraska state recognition for his math results. I was so proud of him and his accomplishment. After having been through losing his father, I would have been very pleased if he was doing average in school, and enjoying life. So I was ecstatic for him to be excelling far beyond average!

And yet, Jon was never boastful about his accomplishments, nor did he ever act like he was better or smarter than anyone in his class. He was simply excited to have had the opportunity to take the test and surprised by the results. There is a social argument behind the idea of a child growing up in a single parent household, exceeding "OK" in order to be an academic scholar. Society simply gives up on these kids and assumes they will not be able to accomplish great things in life. Jon's accomplishment had contradicted that argument, and I firmly believe that his sixth grade teacher played a major role in this accomplishment, based on her constant encouragement and belief in him. We were very fortunate to have had the opportunity for Jon to have her as a teacher, as she left his school the following year to teach in a school closer to her home, similar to what happened with the counselor several years earlier.

> **"Children are likely to live up to what you believe of them."**
>
> - Lady Bird Johnson

If we believe in our children and expect A's and B's on their report cards, and encourage them to work for A's and B's, they are more likely to get them. But if we only expect C's and D's that is probably what they will get since they will have lived up to our expectations of them.

Dr. Ross Pilkington, from the University of Nebraska at Omaha, who presented Encouragement workshops for a number of years and is now retired, reveals the following information about encouragement.

Encouragement focuses on effort – all we can ask of people is 100% effort. If they give that effort, the end result will take care of itself. Whether it is a C in math or an A+ in history, the important factor is the amount of effort put into it.

Praise focuses on the end result – Focusing on the end result can be very discouraging. If you told an athlete, "That 50-yard field goal was great!" the athlete might interpret your statement as, "Now I need to hit a 52-yard field goal to get the coach's praise." It is better to be encouraging.

Encourage the athlete with, "You really worked hard during the week to kick a 50-yard field goal." The athlete has control over the amount of effort he puts forth, but not always over the end result (muddy field, wind, poor center snap, poor hold, etc).

So, focus your efforts on giving encouragement to your kids. Praise may not be a bad thing, but may put too much pressure on them to perform even better next time. (Dreikurs, R., Grunwald, B., and Pepper, F., 1982)

Jon had a baseball coach for a couple of years who was very encouraging to him. He would tell Jon, "You have a heart the size of your whole body, and that is something you can't teach a player. I know that if the ball is hit out to you, you will run it down, and I know that you will always give me 100% effort." Jon is not the fastest player on his team, but I think most coaches respect a player who always gives full effort more than a player who has all the talent in the world, but does not put forth the effort to use it. His baseball coach focused on the effort Jon put forth. He encouraged his effort, and the end result showed it.

Chapter 7

Our Dad

Jon & Natasha's Memories

Jon

My name is Jon Scholz. My dad died when I was 8 years old, and I was in third grade. That morning when my dad left to go to work, he told us that when he died, he would be our guardian angel. That morning, I didn't realize that it would be the last time I talked to my dad. When my dad died the police came to the house, and our mom told us to go up to our rooms.

My sister and I just went into her room and started playing. But after a while we could hear our mom start crying, and I wondered what was wrong. When we went downstairs, she told us what happened, and I was shocked. My uncle, Brian Vanis, arrived and helped us get through it.

My mom and my sister cried a lot, but I didn't seem to cry very much. I guess I just didn't get what happened, and didn't think it could be true. I thought that he was going to be coming back, but little did I know, he wasn't coming back.

When I was little, I wish I could have spent more time with my dad. I guess I just took for granted having a dad. I guess I just never thought what life would be like without one.

My dad really liked history and western movies. His all-time favorites were John Wayne and the show called *Kung Fu*. My dad was also a good artist. I remember once we were playing cards, and we couldn't find the king of hearts. So he just took one of the blank cards and drew a king of hearts on it. I still have that king of hearts, and it is one of the main things that I remember him by.

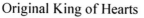
Original King of Hearts   King of Hearts Troy drew

My dad's favorite singer was Jim Croce. He would always play the songs and sing them. Since I wanted to be like him I would try to sing the songs with him. My all-time favorite was "Bad, Bad Leroy Brown." We still have that CD today. As a matter of fact, we like to listen to some of the songs when we have spare time.

Sometimes my dad and I would get some pennies and play poker with each other, and he would let me win other card games. He would also arm wrestle with me all of the time, and he would let me beat him in that also.

My cousins Joe Scholz and Cody Scholz would also help me out by not talking about my dad when I was around. My uncle, Brian Vanis, who was my Confirmation sponsor, seemed like a dad after my dad died. He would make me feel really happy and make me forget about what was going on in my life at the time. After my dad died, he was the person who I always looked up to, and to this day, I still look up to him. The teachers at my school, which was St. Isidore's, were a big help also. They would make learning as comfortable for me as possible. My best friend at the time was Chad Trofholz, he was a big help also. He would be really nice to me and try not to mention anything that would have to do with parents or dads. My mom was a great mom through the whole experience. She handled things well and still does to this day. It really took a strong mom to get through all of this, and I am glad that my mom was there for me, because without her, I wouldn't have been able to get through it all.

Natasha

My name is Natasha Scholz. My dad died when I was 6 years old. My dad and I were very close. I am going to tell you some stories about when my dad was here with us. When my dad died it was January 14, 1995. He died the day before his mom's birthday. He died at work.

The day he died he told us about guardian angels. My first story took place in our car about a week after my dad died. I had a mad look on my face. I said, "Mom, Daddy is in my seat." My mom did not know what to say. Before she could think of something to say, I said, "Oh well, I will just sit on his lap."

Almost every day after my dad died, I would carry his pillow on my head, thinking that he was on the pillow. After he died, I acted like he was there with me every day. Almost every day after he died, I would cry myself to sleep or just cry a lot. Sometimes I would say to my mom, "Mom, I miss Daddy." She would say, "I'll be there in a minute," and she would come and lay down with me until I fell asleep. What was hard for me was when kids would ask me how he died. I would just say I didn't know. Whenever this happened it always made me feel sad.

Since I was in kindergarten, I only went to school half of the day. Since my brother, Jon, was in third grade, he went all day. When Daddy and I would go to pick Jon up from school, I would sing every song I knew. I would sing "Twinkle, Twinkle Little Star," "Mary Had a Little Lamb," "Old McDonald," "The Itsy Bitsy Spider," "Jingle Bells," and the "ABC's," until my brother got out of school. The first day I went to school, I asked my dad if it was the right time to go to school. He said yes, but we were an hour early for school. Every Sunday before church he held me and we danced.

It seemed like every day we had tuna for lunch, especially on Tuesday, which was my dad's day off. One time when I was sick, he made me soup to make me feel better, which he called "Buffalo Butt Stew."

When I went to pre-school I met my best friend Karrie Starzec. She knew that my dad died so she never talked about something to do with my dad or her dad. The day he died Karrie had a birthday party that I was invited to but I couldn't go. Close to the time he died, I had a dance at one of our parks, and I was talking to my friends, and a girl who her dad worked with my dad came up and told me, "Your dad is stupid." I said "Why?" And she said, "Because he shot himself." I told my friends that she was lying, because I did not want them to know. When I got home I told my mom, "Daddy isn't stupid." She responded, "I know. Why would you think that?" Her parents did not tell her not to say things about my dad because it might hurt my feelings. The only thing I wish I could have done was to say good-bye.

When my dad drew the King of Hearts playing card for my brother, he said since he drew the card for Jon, he would make something for me. So he made a stepstool out of carpet and wood so I could reach my clothes hanging in the closet.

One time when our family went to a nice restaurant in Columbus, my dad had a seizure. We were sitting at the table when it happened, and he had a fork and knife in his hands. My mom moved over by my dad and took the fork and knife away so he wouldn't hurt himself or anybody else. I was sitting across from him, and my brother was sitting next to him. When the ambulance got there, they took my dad into a room and laid him on a couch. My mom went with them. While one of the guys from the ambulance took my dad, the other one sat Jon and me at the table and asked us if we were scared. I nodded my head yes. He told us our dad was going to be OK. Then he took us to the room where our mom and dad were. I saw my dad lying on the couch, and I was scared. When he woke up, I gave him a hug, he told me that he was OK and that he loved me. When we got home, I asked my mom what happened. She told me it was a seizure. I asked if he had ever had one before, and she told me he had many, but the one she remembered most was one he had in the shower once. She was downstairs, and if she wouldn't have been there, he might have died.

Chapter 8

Suicide Happens to "normal" Families
Victims and Their Families Are Not Crazy

I recently spoke to a Modern Problems class of high school seniors at the school that Jon and Natasha attend. The class was covering a section on suicide. I was glad to be asked to speak to them, but it saddened me to think that suicide is so common that it is covered in a Modern Problems class. Knowing that suicide will never be eliminated completely, I hope that some day we can reduce the frequency of suicide so that it will no longer be considered a modern problem.

As I prepared to talk to this class, I was concerned about any impact my talk might have on Jon and Natasha. Their school is small enough that undoubtedly someone would make the connection between me and my kids, and I didn't want to cause any negative results for them. I pondered on how to temper this, and here is what I came up with. After telling the students I was asked to talk to them about suicide because my husband committed suicide, I told them, "Some of you may recognize me from seeing me around the community, and you may be thinking to yourself, 'Wow, I didn't realize her husband committed suicide.' And that's a good thing, because I shouldn't look any different than your teachers, your parents, or any other adult you know, because I'm not any different. You shouldn't be able to pick me out of the crowd as being a suicide survivor.

"And some of you may recognize me from seeing me at school events, because my kids go to school here. If you've made the connection between me and my kids, you may be thinking, 'Wow, I didn't realize their dad completed suicide.' And again, that's a good thing, because they shouldn't look any different than any other student here at school, because they aren't any different. You shouldn't be able to pick them out of the crowd as being suicide survivors. Many of you may have experienced the loss of someone you were close to, or may have even experienced a loss through divorce, which is in many ways similar to what we have been through."

Hopefully, this helped the students realize that we are normal people, and that they shouldn't look at us any differently than they would look at anyone else or treat us any differently than they would treat anyone else.

A number of years ago, a friend of mine had a brother who committed suicide. Several years after the suicide, the girl got married. The marriage was probably never meant to be and did not last very long. In the husband's family's attempt to remove themselves from taking the blame for the failed marriage, they told people that it was probably for the best that their son would no longer be married to this girl. After all, they said, her family was psycho because her brother committed suicide. I was appalled at how simple-minded and uncaring this family could be. To accuse an entire family of being psycho just because one member of the family made one very bad decision was beyond comprehension. Is there any family in this world that is perfect? Is there any family without problems of their own? I highly doubt it! Every family has trials and tribulations, and we all hope that people will not condemn us for those trials, but it is so easy to look at someone else's problems and condemn them for theirs.

As I was driving in my car recently, thinking about this, I thought to myself, suicide happens to "normal" families. Just because someone commits suicide does not make that person crazy, and DEFINITELY does not make the remaining family members crazy! Many times after someone commits suicide, it is a total shock to friends and family, because they could not have ever imagined this person being capable of doing it. As I talked at length in Chapter 2, "Why???," depression is almost always one of the key factors involved when someone commits suicide. Just because someone is depressed, does that mean they are psycho? I think not! In fact, those of us who have never felt that level of deep depression should be thanking God that we have never had to experience such a terrible feeling of hopelessness to be in the state of mind they were in to complete suicide.

"Things would be easier if I just died," is probably a thought that has crossed almost every person's mind at one time or another in our lives. But to get to the point where they can complete the act, the person has to be in a terribly depressed state. It is human nature to fight to stay alive, so anyone who commits suicide has to be in an incredibly awful state of mind to be capable of suicide. I, myself, am glad I have never gotten to that state of mind, and I hope I never will.

Besides the fact that Troy was depressed because he did not deal with problems in his life properly, he was a very normal person. He was very well-liked by customers at the store where he worked, especially the kids. Many of the high school-aged kids loved him. He was the type of person who was accepting of everyone. It did not matter to him whether you were white or Hispanic, short or tall, skinny or fat, what type of family you came from, or whether you had a lot of money or not, he looked at the person for who they were. In fact, he usually pulled for the underdog, which meant that many of the kids who did not feel accepted anywhere else, knew they always would be accepted by Troy.

I will always remember one boy in particular who always thought highly of Troy. He was a high school student, and he worked at Pizza Hut. He went into the store where Troy worked a lot. He always told Troy to come to Pizza Hut to eat and he would buy his pizza for him. A couple of times, shortly before Troy died, we finally did go to Pizza Hut when this boy was working. While we were there, he would come out to talk to Troy about every ten minutes to check if everything was OK. He would check if we needed refills on our drinks and if the pizza was done the way we liked it, because he had made it for us himself. Then when we were ready to pay the bill, he would insist that he was going to pay for it. I think Troy may have given him a good deal a few times on some car stereo equipment, and this was his way of paying him back. Unfortunately, the boy died in a tragic car accident after Troy died, but Jon, Natasha and I will always remember him. I am sure Troy greeted him on his entrance to heaven.

While I talked with Barb Wheeler who dealt with suicidal patients for many years, she told me most of the people she worked with were very normal. Once in a while she worked with someone who had problems with schizophrenia. However, most of the time the suicidal patient was a normal person, dealing with some problems in their life not much different than what the rest of us do. They simply had difficulty dealing with those problems. I would like to tell you some of the stories that Ms. Wheeler shared with me.

She told of a man who lost his fiancée to cancer. He was so totally committed to her that in his note he said he took his life in order to be with her for all eternity. Ms. Wheeler said sometimes when there is a cluster suicide, or a group of people who do it together, many times their reasoning is to be together beyond life on earth.

Why is it that a lion tamer can step into a cage with a lion, but if someone else did, they would be torn to shreds. It probably boils down to the treatment of the animal. If the animal feels threatened in any way by the intruder, he will certainly attack back. People will react in much the same way. If they feel threatened, they are likely to attack. Ms. Wheeler shared two stories with me where the person reacted totally different to people who treated them differently. One time she was called to a house where a man had ingested several pills in an attempt to kill himself. When she arrived, she immediately noticed he was a very big man. She described him as having hands like Paul Bunyan. Since he had taken the pills, he was asleep in his bed. With the assistance of a partner from the local military base, she woke him up and asked him if he had taken some pills. After he told her he had, she calmly told him she would like to take him to the hospital and asked if he would go with her. He said he would, and he held her hand as they talked the entire ten-minute ride to the hospital. They did not have any trouble with him until they got to the hospital. When they arrived at the hospital, a young intern walked over to help them. He looked the big man up and down and then told him, "Guys like you are a dime a dozen." After being told this, the man went ballistic. Ms. Wheeler yelled for someone to call for help, because she knew she would not be able to control him. He had been fine until he was mistreated by the intern.

In another case, she was called to a scene where the police had a young man who was holding a knife to his own baby. He had come home that night and was angry about something. He started whipping his wife with a light cord, so she ran out of the house and called the police. Ms. Wheeler said, "He was only holding the knife to the baby to keep the police at bay. I really don't think he would have harmed the baby in any way. I came in and got down on my knees in front of him, and he let his defenses down. I had relinquished power to him. I simply told him he was feeding the baby wrong so it couldn't burp. The baby was lying down. I told him he needed to prop the baby up so he wouldn't get air bubbles in his stomach. He set the knife down and reached out to prop the baby up. My partner grabbed the knife." Again, this man reacted totally different based on the way he was being treated. Just like the lion, if a person feels threatened, they will become much more violent and defensive, whether in the case of an attempted suicide or not.

Ms. Wheeler told another story of a young high school boy who had no relationship with his father, except through guns. His dad taught him how to shoot, even though the boy was scared to death to shoot. The boy was exceptionally scared of one gun in particular. He felt like he could not be a big man to his dad because he did not like to shoot guns. During high school, the boy developed a drug problem, did not get good grades, and had been in trouble at school. Everyone thought he was a problem child, but the last month of his life, he became a good student, quit using drugs, and was doing great. This "problem child" was capable of being "normal," as he proved in his last month. Then just when he seemed to have turned his life around, he shot himself with the gun he was especially afraid of and left a note to his dad that he was finally a man. In the end, his contentedness proves the theory discussed in Chapter 2, "Why???," that many times once a person makes the decision to kill themselves, they are actually happy because they finally feel they are in control of something in their life.

One day Ms. Wheeler received a phone call from some concerned students who noticed a woman sitting in a park crying. When Ms. Wheeler came to talk to her, the woman said her husband had her thrown out of their home and their church. "She could not even attend church, since nobody, not even her own family, would move over to let her sit down. Her husband had been very domineering. She had never been allowed to do anything for herself. Suddenly, she had no home, no family, no church, and no friends, so she took a bunch of pills. She attempted to kill herself, but she survived. She was a beautiful woman, and it was a long road. We had to help her create a whole new life for herself, but thankfully she made it."

As I talked with Ms. Wheeler about her experiences with suicide, she asked me if I think there is ever a case where suicide is justifiable. I told her I did not know if I could ever justify suicide, but that I think I can understand how sometimes a person can get to the point where they see no other option. To justify it would say that I believe it is OK for the person to hurt the people they leave behind by completing suicide, and I cannot bring myself to do that.

I had the opportunity to talk with another woman whose husband committed suicide, only under very different circumstances than mine. It was obvious to me that this was a very "normal" family, simply caught up in the stresses and pressures of corporate America. Some of her story is shared in the following paragraphs.

A promotion within the husband's company required the family to move to another state, which turned out to be very hard on the family. "My husband had always been the strong one. He was the type of person you could always count on. He had always taken responsibility. When he sensed trouble, he always tried to mend it." But when work pressures got to be too much, and he felt the need to choose between his family and his job, it was a 'no-win' situation, as he loved his family and his job both very much.

"Everyone was in shock when they learned that he committed suicide. Nobody could believe he could do this. He was just not the type to commit suicide. He was so 'normal'. From an outsider's view, he appeared to have everything—a beautiful wife and family, great job, plenty of money, nice house, and nice cars. What more could anyone want? Everyone thought we were a very happy family.

"When my husband died, it felt like my heart got ripped in half. With time, though, our hearts get filled up with other things. After the first few days following a death, all of our friends and family resume their normal lives. They have no choice. They have to continue with their lives. The people who experienced the loss, however, have to create a new 'normal'. Normal now has to exist without their loved one. People used to ask me how I was doing. That is a difficult question to answer when your heart has just been ripped out. I would simply tell them, 'I am doing the best I can.' With that, they were not under the false impression that everything was great, but they knew I was trying my best to get through it.

"The first Christmas season after my husband's death, which was only a few months later, I felt like a ghost in the shopping malls. I wanted to walk up to people and say, 'Don't you know what's just happened to me?' After time, when I met someone on the street, I would think, 'I wonder what your story is.' We all have our stories behind the masks that we wear.

"The year after my husband's death, we decided to move back 'home'. We felt that it would be good to return to our circle of friends. We returned as different people, however, so it was difficult going back to our old friends.

"After our return, one of the couple friends that my husband and I used to get together with invited me out to dinner with them. When they arrived to pick me up, my friend got in the back seat and allowed me to sit in the front seat with her husband. After 23 years of marriage, it was very difficult to go places and do things we would normally have done together. It was like there was a void that could not be filled. Something as simple as allowing me to sit in the front seat of the car was one of the nicest things anybody has done for me since this happened. She knew that she would have her husband to go home with, so she allowed me those few minutes to have someone by my side rather than sitting in the back seat alone.

"Since this happened, I have had people tell me they knew someone else who committed suicide, so I could talk to them. It was like saying, 'Since you're willing to talk about it, we can too.' Suicide is not an easy subject to talk about openly because of the social stigma. But for those who have experienced it firsthand, it is nice to be able to talk to someone who understands what it is like to go through it.

"The holidays, of course, are always difficult. During the holidays, we light a candle to symbolize that his presence is with us."

My Mom and Dad's reaction

As I mentioned earlier, my mom and dad had no idea there were even any problems in my marriage, and they definitely did not expect Troy to be capable of suicide. We had done a good job of "covering up" for them over the years, and Troy never appeared to be suicidal to them. This was their reaction.

"As Barb's parents, we were really surprised when we got the call from our son, Brian, on a Saturday morning telling us that our daughter wanted to see us. 'We were planning to come over this afternoon anyway,' we answered. 'I think you should come now,' he said, so we dropped everything and drove the 25 miles to see her, all the way wondering what was awaiting us. Brian had dropped no hints. We imagined our grandson or granddaughter getting hurt, or our daughter or son-in-law getting hurt. Most every kind of emergency crossed our minds, but never once did we come close to imagining what had happened. When we arrived and Brian told us that our son-in-law had taken his life, it devastated us. We had no clue this sort of thing could happen. Looking back, we realize that we should have recognized some signs. We wish our daughter had told us about more of their problems. We realize that she was shielding us, but being older, we think we may have realized that they needed professional help. One thing is certain, a person with this frame of mind cannot understand the need for, or type of help needed to combat this depression. I guess we're trying to say, 'There are times when we should swallow our pride and ask for help, for ourselves or for anyone unable to recognize their great need.

"We loved our son-in-law dearly, and only wish we could have done something to prevent this terrible tragedy from happening. We are very consoled that there are great counselors who work so well with the struggling family after they suffer such a loss. We feel that due to these well-trained, caring people, our daughter and her children have been able to restructure their lives remarkably well. We will always have fond memories of our son-in-law, and are so pleased that Barb, Jon and Natasha have been helped to recall so many of the good times with their husband and father."

"I don't know the key to success, but the key to failure is trying to please everybody."

— Bill Cosby

Maybe this was the problem with both Troy and me, always wanting to please everybody. For the years that I was unhappy in my marriage, I never wanted anyone to know it. I did not want to upset or disappoint Troy, Jon, Natasha, my family, his family, the church, or anyone. I did not want any of them to think we were failing. So instead of confronting the problem like I should have, I held it all inside until I could not hold it in any more. I wanted everyone to think we had a successful marriage, but instead of admitting the truth and asking for help, I ended up failing because of my attempt to please everybody.

Troy was also the type who always wanted to please everybody. Many times he would allow himself to be taken advantage of, just to keep peace and make everyone happy. We are never going to please everyone all of the time, so as long as we are doing things that are pleasing to God and to ourselves, that is the main thing we need to be concerned about. If we get too consumed by trying to please everyone else, we will surely fail since we cannot please everyone all of the time.

As Dr. Pilkington puts it, "Pleasers are often very discouraged people. They try to please everyone and they fail. Failure leads to discouragement. Pleasers also suffer from 'please fatigue.' It takes a lot of energy to try to please everyone. They have little energy for themselves. It's OK to please others but is also OK to please yourself."

Other "normal" families

Several other stories have been shared with me, each indicating that suicide happens to "normal" families. I would like to share these stories with you, to provide different perspectives, and to further prove that suicide does not just happen in families checking in and out of the psych ward of the hospital.

One story is: "I once had a co-worker who was a good man and who worshiped his son. He could not stop talking about how wonderful his son was. His wife, however, made more money than he did and held it over his head. One morning he called work and said he would be in later than normal. We found out that afternoon that he had driven his car head on into a truck, and we were convinced that it was a suicide in disguise. We could not understand how he could leave his son when he obviously loved him very much. He could not have thought about the impact on those left behind at all or he could not have done it. He was a good person, and we could not imagine him wanting to leave his son. He must have been very distraught to be able to leave him."

Another story is: "When I was a sophomore in high school, there was a new girl who moved to our school. She started dating one of our other classmates who ended up quitting school. When she broke up with him, he committed suicide. Nobody would have suspected that he was capable of this. We all questioned what we could have done to prevent it."

Another story is: "I knew a couple where the husband had the misfortune of ill health and could no longer work. He had tried to talk his wife into committing suicide together with him. One day, as she was leaving to go to the grocery store, he asked if she wanted him to go with her. When she told him she did not need him to go, he perceived it to mean that he was of no use. Since she would not commit suicide with him, he finally did it himself."

As these stories demonstrate, suicide can and DOES happen in "normal" families. Many times the problems being experienced are no different than what any normal family experiences. So why does it happen in some families and not others? Probably for a combination of reasons, but one common thread is depression. Some people deal with the stresses in life better than others. When someone does not deal with those stresses very well, it can overwhelm them until they see no other way out.

I am in no way suggesting that suicide is normal, or that it is the right thing to do when you feel overwhelmed with life's stresses. I am simply saying that it can happen in a very normal family, and that just because one person in a family may have committed suicide, that does not mean everyone in the family is suicidal.

Chapter 9

Is there such a thing as "proper" and "improper" grieving?

Everyone Grieves Differently, So Nobody Can Tell You How

About 3½ years after Troy died, another terrible tragedy occurred in our town of approximately 20,000 people. I came to work one morning to find out that a woman who worked in the same department as I did had apparently been a victim of a murder-suicide committed by her husband that morning. I had felt like I was doing pretty good, like I was getting back to normal, or at least as much as I ever would be. But that morning, when I heard the news, it was like being hit by a semi-truck all over again. I remember having the same "numb" feeling again all through my body. It felt as though every ounce of blood was flushed right out of me. I was in total shock and disbelief. I didn't even know this man, but I was angry toward him. How could he have done something like this? It was hard enough to accept someone taking their own life, but how could he take someone else with him because of his own misery?

This was very difficult for me to deal with. First of all, it brought back a lot of memories for me that I had no longer been dealing with on a daily basis. Second, it reminded me of how I felt immediately after learning of Troy's death. When Troy died, my initial feeling, of course, was one of shock and disbelief, hoping that somehow I could "fix" or reverse what happened. Once reality set in, though, I prayed, "Thank you, God, that Troy wasn't selfish enough to take me and/or the kids with him." I knew that could have happened, since someone in a suicidal state is not thinking clearly anyway. In fact, within months of Troy's death, there was a multiple murder-suicide in our town where the husband killed his wife, two children, and then himself. It had definitely crossed my mind numerous times, that things could have happened to me the same way.

As I mentioned earlier, I hadn't even thought about these feelings for several years, but when the murder-suicide occurred, it was as if I was going through it all over again. I made a comment to a friend, who had known the husband involved in the most recent incident, that I just kept thinking the same thing could have happened to me. She really caught me by surprise when she told me that I needed to quit thinking that way. I know she meant well by her comment, just wanting me to feel better, but this troubled me, as I thought, "Maybe I AM dragging this out. Maybe I AM dwelling on this too long. Maybe I DO need to just get over it!" But I wanted to know if what I was feeling was normal. Was I losing it, or was what I was experiencing OK? Luckily for me, my employer made available a counselor from the Employee Assistance Program for anyone who needed to talk to someone about what happened. So I decided to take advantage of the opportunity to talk to someone who had studied what was considered to be "normal."

I explained the entire situation to her, starting with Troy's death, and then sharing how this recent incident made me feel. How it had brought a lot of memories back, especially the feeling that I could have been taken with him. Then I asked her if I was dwelling on the past, if I needed to put it behind me and move on. I was relieved to hear her say that it is very normal to relive certain aspects of a traumatic experience when a similar incident occurs.

Many times when we talk about grief, several stages are mentioned. Those stages again as referenced in Chapter 1 are Denial, Anger or Resentment, Bargaining, Depression and finally Acceptance. The counselor shared some very logical concepts with me. It was some of the most helpful information I have received. She said that the stages of grief often talked about are simply a reference point, and that every person goes through those stages differently. Not every person will experience every one of the stages, and when we do go through them, we will do so in varying degrees.

One person may experience only a brief period of anger, but remain in the denial stage for a long while. The next person may not even experience denial, but will do a lot of bargaining. We may experience those stages in a different order than a friend or family member does. We might go through a stage, and then come back some time later, and go through that same stage again.

All of this made perfect sense and explained why I was feeling the way I was feeling when the murder-suicide occurred so long after my personal experience. What a relief! I WAS OK... I WAS normal!

Here are some examples of "normal" patterns of grief.

Mary

Mary may experience 1 week of Denial, then 1 month of Anger and 1 year of Depression. Then something triggers another week of Anger until she reaches Acceptance for 6 months. She falls back into Depression for 3 months before returning to Acceptance forever.

1. Denial – 1 week
2. Anger – 1 month
3. Depression – 1 year
4. Anger – 1 week
5. Acceptance – 6 months
6. Depression – 3 months
7. Acceptance - forever

Steve

Steve may have 3 days in Denial, followed by a week of Bargaining, 3 months of Depression, 3 weeks of Anger and back to Depression for a month. He then gets stuck in the Anger stage so that he never reaches Acceptance.

1. Denial – 3 days
2. Bargaining – 1 week
3. Depression – 3 months
4. Anger – 3 weeks
5. Depression – 1 month
6. Anger - forever

The bottom line is, we all experience grief in our own individual ways, and on our own time schedules. The most important thing to understand is that whatever stage or feeling we are experiencing, we need to allow ourselves to go through it rather than trying to pretend it is not there. If we suppress our feelings of grief, we will only force ourselves to take longer to get through that stage and move on. That is, if we are lucky enough to be able to move on and not get stuck in that stage forever. Have you ever met anyone who is eternally bitter or angry over the loss of a loved one? No matter how much we would like to bring our loved one back, we cannot. The best we can do is to continue on with our own lives. You cannot do that if you allow yourself to get stuck in a stage simply because you refuse to let yourself experience your feelings of anger, denial, or whatever the case might be.

So please listen to your heart. Allow yourself to feel and experience whatever it is that you are feeling or experiencing, at whatever time you are feeling or experiencing it. It may be easier at the time to push things into the closet and ignore them, but believe me, down the road, you will be much better off if you allow yourself to go through it.

This means you must also respect the feelings of your family and friends. Please remember that they are not you. They are their own person, with their own feelings and their own grieving process. Do not expect them to grieve on the same schedule as you. Allow them to grieve in their own way and in their own time, and never tell someone else how they should grieve.

Grief and Grief Processing

In the past, grief has gotten some bad press, that it is something to be avoided. However, grief is not a negative thing unless you let it become negative. Grief can be a very positive thing if you become stronger because of your grief experiences. I would now like to share some grief processing concepts that were provided to me by Dr. Ross Pilkington, intermixed with several personal stories about our experiences with the loss of Troy.

Grief is a lifelong process with different degrees of severity. It is usually related to a major crisis in life. In reality, however, life deals us small grief experiences every day. These small experiences give us practice to develop our grief processing skills needed for the major crises we will face in our lives. (Bichekas, Georgia, 1986)

Some examples of small doses of grief may be the death of a pet, TV shows that triggers grief within us, a book we read that causes grief, when the doctor tells you that you can no longer eat tomatoes and you love tomatoes, or when a friend moves away to another city. Grief includes every day small grief experiences and occasional large grief experiences.

Grief is a process, a natural emotional reaction to a loss. Your grief reaction varies due to the kind of loss you are experiencing and the degree of that loss. Mourning is a cultural response to a loss. Mourning involves acting as society expects you to act. Society expects you to be sad and to express your sadness by crying. Bereavement is a state of having suffered a loss, and the period of time you are in that state. It is the time and what you do in that time.

Losses can be real/physical, or they can be symbolic. A real loss is losing a desired possession or person. A symbolic loss, on the other hand, may involve a divorce or loss of stature through a demotion at work. A symbolic loss is many times not seen as a loss to society, but it is definitely still a loss. When people go to a counselor they are grieving. They have lost their ability to cope, they have lost part of themselves, lost their ability to make decisions and solve problems.

Grief work is a process of letting go of what was and preparing for what is to come. "Grief work" best describes counseling the grieving, because it IS work. It is hard work. It takes time, it takes a process, and it takes monitoring.

When Freud talked about grief in 1917, he said it comes from a loss, and not just a death. It is a normal process in which self-healing is important. It is a departure from normal life because it is a painful dejection, causes a loss of the capacity to love, causes a decrease in activity and a decreased interest in the outside world.

Eric Lindemann, author of *Crisis Intervention*, has studied loss reactions, and found that the mind has the ability to make the body sick. Through his studies, he identified three tasks that a person needs to go through in their grief work. He says the most important and difficult of the three is emancipation from bondage of the person who was lost. This involves untying the ties that bind. This does not mean the person is forgotten, nor are they no longer loved. It is merely reinvesting your energy in others.

The second task Lindemann identified is readjustment to the environment in which the person who was lost is absent from or missing. This involves reviewing memories and feelings connected with the lost person or object. The third task is the formation of new relationships. (Bichekas, Georgia, 1987)

Without ever having heard about these concepts at the time when Jon, Natasha and I were experiencing our grief, I firmly believe in them. I believe that doing the things Lindemann describes helped us tremendously in our path to recovery. We talk about Troy on a regular basis in a loving manner. Whenever a story comes up or something that triggers a memory of an event or something he had done, we share the stories and memories. We do not ever try to sweep anything under the rug. I think many times when someone loses a loved one there is a tendency to not talk about that person because it is perceived that it is disrespectful or that it is just too painful. Unfortunately, it becomes much more painful over time if it is bottled up inside. I believe it also turns things into a negative instead of a positive. If it is treated as if it is a "hush, hush" topic of discussion, how can the grieving person remember their lost loved one with a sense of joy, and keep the memory of that person alive? I believe this causes you to have a more difficult time getting over the anger you experience, and could cause you to be eternally bitter rather than remembering the person with love. This is probably even more important in the case of a suicide than in any other case, since there may be a tendency to have more anger toward the lost loved one than in other types of death anyway.

I have always felt that it was very important to our recovery that we talk about Troy in a loving manner, and that we remember all of the good times we spent together, and the wonderful traits that he had. It would serve no good purpose to discuss negative traits, or to be bitter toward him for what he did. Therefore, I always encourage Jon and Natasha to never forget their Dad, and that we will always love him even though he is no longer with us. Yes, it may have been difficult and uncomfortable to talk about him and our memories of him at first, but each time we did, it got easier. In fact, now when we talk about him, it is always with smiles on our faces, and many times a chuckle to accompany the smiles. What started out to be somewhat difficult has actually turned out to be very therapeutic. Many times, as adults, we think we need to "protect" the kids from thinking about their lost loved one, but are we really protecting them or hurting them further by not allowing them to share and hang on to their memories of the one who died? Natasha was probably the best of all of us to start talking about Troy and her memories of him, and she still does today. What better gift could we give to our loved one than to always carry on their memory after they are gone from this life? Troy will never really die until everyone that knew him dies. Memory is one gift from God that death cannot destroy.

Dr. Pilkington shared with me something that helped his family when his wife passed away. Since she knew that she was dying, she left the family with four requests.

1. Remember the good times.
2. Don't give up on God.
3. Help each other out.
4. Go on with your lives.

This helped the family with their recovery. She became a model for them and it worked. In Chapter 11 you will see how Troy became a model for us also, and it worked for us as well.

Talking about our lost loved one allows us to reduce emotional flooding. It helps us control emotions and become more rational and logical because of the constructive thinking that results from talking. Then we are not so emotionally flooded and driven but cognitively driven.

Being able to talk about our loved ones is a lesson that I actually learned many years earlier when my grandpa passed away. Grandpa was a very stern man, who kids did not want to cross. When he laid down the law, you knew he meant business. On the other hand, he had a heart of gold and would have given the shirt off his back to someone in need. Grandpa loved *All In the Family*, the Archie Bunker TV show, and *All Star Wrestling*. I remember countless Sunday mornings when Grandpa and Grandma came to our house for dinner, and Grandpa would sit on the edge of his seat watching All Star Wrestling. Hulk Hogan would body slam his opponent, jump in the air and come down on him with his knee in his chest. Grandpa would rock back in his chair with one hand over his well-fed belly and the other hand over his mouth as he laughed his wheezy, squeaky laugh. His eyes would squint and he would laugh to the point of tears. He always proclaimed All Star Wrestling to be the best "acting" on television, as he watched it for comedic purposes.

Grandpa would also rock back in his chair as he watched Edith Bunker come squealing out of the kitchen with an ice-cold can of beer for Archie. As Archie grumbled some slam to his son-in-law, Michael, Grandpa would again laugh, as Edith would say "Oh, ARCHIE!!!" My brothers and sister and I would just look at each other and snicker as we enjoyed watching Grandpa's reactions.

Grandpa loved telling personal stories as well, some dating back decades. He would tell the same stories over and over, many of them about my brothers and sister and I. We must have heard him tell the same stories hundreds of times, but it was always enjoyable to watch and listen to him tell those stories because of the way he told them. It was fun just to see how much he enjoyed telling the stories each time, as he squinted his eyes shut, he laughed so hard. I only wish we would have snuck a tape player under the table for one of our family meals together so we could replay his stories and his memory.

Grandpa died of a sudden massive heart attack in January of 1990. For Grandpa, it was the best way to go. He probably would not have made a very good patient if he had to lie in a hospital bed, suffering for months. Grandpa had been very active up until the day he died at the age of 81. It would have driven him insane to lie in a bed, helpless. For the rest of us, though, it was a total shock. Grandpa had hardly ever been sick in his life, and there was certainly no warning for us that he was going to die.

The evening of the wake service, after the prayers were said, and the family was together at the funeral home, my sister Geri and I were standing around crying over the loss of Grandpa. Our older brother, Jay, came over to us and started telling the old stories that Grandpa would tell, and saying, "Remember when Grandpa said.....," or "Remember when Grandpa did......" Geri and I looked at each other and then at Jay; we told him he was being disrespectful to stand there and laugh when Grandpa was barely even gone. We expected the cultural response to Grandpa's death from Jay, which is mourning, sadness and crying.

Jay looked us square in the eye and said, "No. Grandpa wouldn't want us to stand around crying and mourning because he is gone. He would want us to remember the good times we shared with him. He would want us to celebrate his life, not his death, and to smile and laugh when we think about him." I have carried those thoughts with me ever since Grandpa's death, because Jay was right.

I will always be thankful for the message from God, delivered through my brother, that when we lose someone we love, we should celebrate their life, not their death, and cherish the memories we have with them.

The Word Suicide

Although I feel it is very important to talk about our lost loved ones, one thing that has always been difficult for me is to actually say Troy "committed suicide." Whenever someone finds out that my husband passed away, of course they will ask what happened, expecting that he had cancer or was in a car accident. It has been several years since Troy died, and I still have a hard time saying those words. I think it is because the word *suicide*, to me, is a negative word. People do not think about suicide in a positive light, but a negative one. I do not want people to think of Troy in a negative light or that he was a bad person for what he did, so I would always refer to his death as "He took his own life." I think this phrase sounds much softer and invokes a feeling of sorrow rather than anger. It was simply easier for me to verbalize it this way.

When I talked with Barb Wheeler about her experiences with suicide, it was not long into the conversation when she said she prefers to use the phrase "completed suicide" rather than "committed suicide." They really mean the same thing, but saying the person completed suicide simply says they followed through with the act. "Committed" she said, "is a term used in conjunction with a crime." Therefore, completed sounds much less accusatory and negative than committed. I agreed with her logic. Except for the rare case where the suicide victim takes others with them, the only crime committed by the person is against themselves by cheating themselves out of the rest of their life.

There is a restaurant in the city where I live that has a wonderful dessert tray, with various flavors of cheesecake, pie and cake. Several months after Troy died, I went to this restaurant with a group of friends to celebrate one of their birthdays. We enjoyed our lunch, and when finished, the waitress came over with the dessert tray and began naming all of the options on the tray. There was a really scrumptious looking piece of chocolate cake, overflowing with cholesterol and calories. It had two layers and thick chocolate frosting, and I had my eye on it. It looked wonderful, and I was planning to order it. When she got to that item on the dessert tray, she said, "And this is the chocolate suicide cake." It did not matter how good that cake looked, there was no way I was going to order it now. First of all, I could not verbalize the name of the item. Secondly, I thought it was extremely insensitive for them to name a dessert after suicide. The thought that they would take suicide so lightly that their chocolate cake was worth completing suicide over was appalling! I was very offended, and it took me a long time before I could watch that dessert tray go by or see it coming to my table without becoming very uncomfortable.

Since I started writing this book, when people ask me what my book will be about, I have had no choice but to tell them it is about healing after a suicide. The first few times I told someone that, it was very difficult and uncomfortable for me to say. I have found, however, that each time I say the word *suicide* it becomes easier. I believe the more we talk about the entire situation, the more it becomes fact and it becomes less emotional. Sometimes we need to tell our story over and over before we accept it and/or become more comfortable with it. This is called catharsis, which by Webster's definition means, "a relieving of the emotions."

One day Jon told me that someone at school, who didn't know Troy had died, asked him where his dad lived. That made Jon uncomfortable because he did not know how to respond. I explained to him my discomfort with the phrase "committed suicide," and that I understood if he was uncomfortable saying it also. I told him that if it was easier for him, like it was for me, he could tell them that, "He took his own life." However, it was also OK for him to just tell them that he did not want to talk about it. I told him that most kids would not push for more if he said he did not want to talk about it, but if they did push for more, and he was uncomfortable telling them his dad committed suicide, to just say "He took his own life."

This helped him develop a plan for the next time someone asked him about his dad. He would be prepared for it rather than being caught off-guard, not knowing what to say. It does not seem to bother him any more when someone asks him about his dad, or at least he does not sit and worry that someone will ask a question. Dr. Pilkington teaches his students that when a client leaves their counseling office, they need a plan to follow for the next week. They need a plan to change, to cope, to take action or for whatever reason, but people need a plan. If they have a plan, they are less likely to get lost along the way.

Manifestation of grief reactions

There are psychological, physiological and social manifestations of the grief responses, also provided by Dr. Ross Pilkington. (Bichekas, Georgia, 1987)

Psychological manifestation

1. Avoidance

Your world is shaken and overcome by impact. As the body goes into shock, so does the psyche. It is a natural response to the powerful impact of the loss. Confusion is the result, and you may be "dazed." You cannot hurt that much right away so you are protected by the avoidance phase of the psychological manifestation. Denial is a form of avoidance. It is necessary and therapeutic. It is a buffer for our psyche, allowing us to work through our grief a little bit at a time. There is disbelief and a need to know why. For the quiet person, it shows up as withdrawal. For an outgoing person, it appears as outbursts.

2. Confrontation

This is the emotional phase when the grief is confronted. You accept what has happened, and anger develops from it. We do not like it when something has been taken from us. The Confrontation phase may consist of the following feelings.

Anger – How much we loved the lost one will determine the amount of anger we have. "I promised to love you forever and my forever is not up yet." Some people will hide anger because society says anger is bad. Some will have misplaced anger at other people or things.

Guilt – Some people may suffer from a lot of guilt. They may have guilt about being angry. They may have guilt about the relationship not being well defined. "How much did I love this person?" There may be feelings that you did not do all you should have done. You may have survival guilt, "I should have died and they should have lived." You may feel guilty about being sad or crying.

Depression and despair – People become depressed and withdrawn, which is a form of regression. Depression and anger team up to be a good case of anxiety and anxiety attacks.

Confrontation is an intense stage for psychological manifestations. We confront the loss and are pre-occupied with the loss. Visual and/or auditory hallucinations can occur. We may see or hear the lost person, and it seems like a dream. You may wonder if you can cross over back to reality. You focus a lot on the lost person and your senses pick up on that. You can feel, hear, smell and see the lost person. If this happens to

119

you, you are NOT going crazy! These things can and DO happen. If you have some hallucinations you are not crazy. If you perceive yourself as going crazy you will only become more depressed and the grieving process slows down.

3. Reestablishment

In this phase, there is a gradual decline in grief as you re-enter the world and learn to live with the loss. The loss is not forgotten but put into its proper place. You can now remember your lost loved one, but without tears. Guilt could appear in the early reestablishment phase. We may have guilt about recovering from the loss, guilt about feeling better, and seeing recovery as an act of betrayal. We finally break the ties that bind us but still love the lost person.

Physiological manifestation

The physiological manifestation is brought about by the emotional response to the loss. It is the same as stress responses but more severe in grief. The physiological results may be eating disorders, weight loss, weight gain, or sleeping disorders. You may do a lot of sighing, which is a breathing behavior that reduces stress and allows you to calm down. You may experience restlessness, pacing and searching to find the lost person or pacing to search for comfort. You burn off the energy you generate, thus you may become tired and worn out.

Social manifestation

Some of the social effects are dependent on societal factors, cultural factors, religious factors and external support systems.

Types of grief

There are many different types of grief we may experience, reasons for failure to grieve, reasons we get "stuck" in grief, and factors affecting each individual's grief responses, again provided to me by Dr. Ross Pilkington. (Bichekas, Georgia, 1987)

Abnormal or exaggerated grief – is prolonged grief with intense manifestations. This person suffers from over-guilt. They may take on some of the symptoms of the lost person, such as illnesses if the person had been sick. They may also take on some personal traits of the person, such as quotes/sayings, quirks, mannerisms that the lost person displayed.

Normal grief – usually takes a year but can go on as long as three years. Acute grief occurs during the first 6 months and less grief the last 6 months of the first year. Normal grief usually takes a minimum of a year because it takes a year to go through all of the seasons, anniversaries and birthdays that had been spent with the lost person. After a maximum of three years, reestablishment should be complete.

Abbreviated grief – is a short period of grief but very genuine. It is caused by expedient replacement of the lost loved one or insufficient attachment to them in the first place.

Inhibited grief – occurs when the person does not follow the normal grief pattern. The grief process or healing is inhibited so the person suffers psychosomatic illness. When this happens, physical illness may be brought on by emotions.

Delayed grief – is when normal grief is delayed for years and then kicked into more grief when another loss occurs. Grief may be delayed for the person who takes care of everyone else during the actual crisis. The "macho" person may suffer delayed grief, since they may not want anyone to think they are weak enough to grieve, so they suppress their grieving. By not allowing themselves to grieve at the time of the event, they may cause themselves to go through Inhibited grief, and eventually through Delayed grief.

Anticipatory grief – may occur when there is an expected loss. At the time of the actual loss, the grief is abbreviated or less. This may also be called "pre-trauma" grief. The problem with this type of grief is you may have already suffered from a long grief period (exaggerated grief) prior to the Anticipatory grief. This happened with many of the POWs who returned to the US. Families and friends had grieved and reestablished and made the detachments with the lost people, who then returned. This caused a high divorce rate.

Some additional results of any type of abnormal grief, not already mentioned are over activity without a sense of loss, social isolation, and extreme hostility toward others, especially the doctor or psychologist. You may develop the "wooden structure syndrome," where you look like wood with no facial expressions in order to mask the grief. You may have agitated depression with tension, insomnia, inferiority and thoughts of suicide yourself. Some of these abnormal grief tendencies may appear in normal grief as well. They usually appear in response to an absence of grief, to prolonged grief or to distorted grief.

There are two conditions that may cause trouble for a person who is working their way through their grief.

1. The mourner's difficulty in tolerating the emotional distress of grief.

2. The mourner's extreme need to continue the relationship with the lost person. It is common and normal to desire to keep the relationship but some NEED it to an extreme.

There are numerous **reasons for failure to grieve** which lead to abnormal grieving. (Bichekas, Georgia, 1987)

1. Social negation of the loss. Things that are not seen as losses in society but are, such as abortion, miscarriage, giving a child up for adoption.

2. Socially unacceptable losses, such as drug overdose deaths, suicide, murder and HIV/AIDS.

3. Geographical distance from support systems, or none available at all. This may be especially true for the elderly population where all of their supporters have died.

4. You are the caretaker of the other family members, the "macho" person who got everyone else through the crisis.

5. Ambivalence about the relationship. You do not know how much to grieve because you do not know how much you loved the person.

6. Loss is an extension of a loss of self for the person who was extremely dependent on the lost person.

7. Being overwhelmed by multiple losses, such as a murder-suicide.

8. Grieving is peculiar to a person's private logic. You cannot grieve because it is a sign of weakness. "If I start crying, I will never stop."

There are also many reasons why people **get "stuck" in their process of grieving** and never get to Acceptance. (Bichekas, Georgia, 1987)

1. Refusing to acknowledge the loss, denial. Go on with life without grieving as if it did not happen.

2. Focusing on what was lost. This is the doom and gloom approach. "I'm a victim" "Isn't it awful" thoughts forever and ever. This person is in a bad emotional state with no signs of improvement.

3. Hurrying into a new beginning, rebound relationships. We may escape the pain by getting into a new relationship too soon. If this happens, problems may return later if the person never experienced their grief. There may be a poor adjustment to the new because the old has not been processed yet.

4. We are not sure how we feel about the lost person and deciding delays recovery.

There are several things adults can do **to not get "stuck"** in our grieving process. (Bichekas, Georgia, 1987)

1. Select a model for grief work and follow it. The Transition Model is presented in Chapter 5, and Dr. Kubler-Ross's Stages of grief are described in Chapter 1 and discussed throughout the book.

2. Recognize the loss.

3. Be honest with yourself. It hurts but it will get better.

4. Allow yourself to experience the pain. Do not try to mask it.

5. Find other reasons to live. Whatever it is that is important to you; work, God, family, hope for new relationships, and so forth. Determine what those reasons are and focus on them.

6. Share your grief with others. Whether through a counselor, a friend who is an open listener, support groups or family, your grief needs to be shared with someone.

7. Take care of yourself because you deserve it. 40-80% of survivors of the death of a spouse either die themselves or have serious health problems within two years. If you do not take care of yourself, the result could be depression, alcoholism, heart problems, or psychological problems.

8. Dump your imagined guilt. The death was not your fault so don't own it.

9. Do not make serious decisions after a loss, such as moving, selling things, changing jobs, etc.

10. Discover your strengths. Do a self-inventory, and use your strengths in your recovery.

There are also many **factors affecting** each individual's **grief responses**. (Bichekas, Georgia, 1987)

1. The nature or meaning of the relationship with the person.

   What the loss means to you is a key factor. For example, if a runner is told he cannot run any more, the loss of that activity is devastating. If a non-runner is told they cannot run, it is no big deal. Therefore, you cannot use your own standards to judge what a loss means to another person.

2. Individual qualities of the relationship with the person.

   If a dysfunctional family with alcoholism, physical, mental or sexual abuse was involved, you may react differently to the loss.

3. Personality and coping ability of the griever.

   If you run from life, you will run from grief also. If you give up in small crises, you will give up in the loss of a person. If you drink when small crises hit, you will get drunk when a large one does. Your coping strategies used in life will be used with the loss of a loved one also.

4. Past experiences with death.

   What was used in a previous death situation will be used again. If past experience was a negative one, the present one likely will be also.

5. Level of maturation and intelligence.

   More mature or intelligent people grieve better than immature people or less intelligent people.

6. Age of the person lost and type of person they were.

It is easier for us when an older person dies because they have "lived life." Grief is much more difficult when someone dies young, especially our own child.

7. Griever's perception of the person's lost fulfillment in life.

    "They had so much they wanted to accomplish," or "They will never get to see their kids grow up and get married."

8. The Death Surround - the immediate circumstances of the death.

    Location – the family surrounded for support vs. death happened far away

    Reason – natural or suicide/murder

    Degree of preparation – was it expected or unexpected

    Suffering – was there suffering or no suffering

    Medical care – best or poor

    The amount of unfinished business between the person lost and the griever

The effects of drugs and medications

Sedatives can be prescribed to help you through the grief, but they slow down the grief process. They slow down the body and the mind, and are usually more negative than positive. Unfortunately, pain is mother nature's way of healing, but with sedatives the griever does not experience the pain. If you were drugged during the funeral, the funeral did not serve its purpose of helping you finalize the death. The funeral is a support system and the griever does not use this system if they are drugged.

Some medications are helpful. Those medications that keep you strong and healthy, with regular sleeping and eating patterns are important for your strength to grieve. (Bichekas, Georgia, 1987)

Chapter 10

Helping/Counseling the Griever
Others Need Help Too

Not only may you be grieving yourself, but you may need to help someone else through their grieving as well. We all have encountered a friend or relative who is grieving, and sometimes we feel at a loss for how to help. Should we talk about it? Should we change the subject? What practical things can we do to make a difference? Some ways you can help someone get through the grieving process follow. Some of this information was received from the Methodist Employee Assistance Program and reprinted with their permission.

Listening: The griever needs to be listened to in order to vent their feelings and review their relationship with the lost one in a non-judgmental environment. This helps the griever get over emotional ties to the lost person and to disconnect from what was in order to live with what is. Encourage the griever to begin to grieve NOW, with you, to vent, talk about their grief and the lost loved one. The gift of listening means opening our hearts to what the other has to say. It means truly hearing what is being said instead of using the time to formulate a response. When the bereaved knows they can trust someone with their pain, fear and anger, they have found a wonderful resource on the way to healing.

Eric Lindemann suggested three phases of venting.

1. Review the relationship

2. Express sorrow of the loss

3. Verbalize the guilt about the "shoulds"

Presence: Be present, both physically and emotionally, immediately after the death and for months after the loss, because grief work takes time. It does not happen overnight, and even though you may not always see the signs outwardly, the person grieving may still need someone to talk to or "vent" with. You may not have a lot to say, you may not know what to say, but simply "being with" is important.

Assistance: During the shock and disorientation phase, identify someone to do the daily chores for the person, such as going to the bank or the grocery store, cleaning the bathroom, house sitting during the visitation, baby-sitting during the funeral, or providing dinner during the visitation. Whatever you can or will do, be specific in your offer. "Let me know if there's anything I can do," is not specific.

Resilience: As the shock of the death wears off and friends or relatives move into a period of numbness, we may sense that they are avoiding or turning down offers of help and support. Continue to offer that support. Make periodic phone calls. Drop a card. Stop by for a visit. Be persistent without being intrusive. Bereaved people need support, even though sometimes they are unaware of that need.

Acceptance: The griever will experience anger: anger at the loved one for dying, anger at others whose lives are still "normal," anger at God for allowing this painful event into their life. Get the griever to express and accept their feelings. Be permissive and non-judgmental. They are judging themselves anyway, and do not need any help from others. Let them review, cry and talk, and allow them to repeat, REPEAT, **REPEAT!!** Listening non-judgmentally to the anger provides a safe place to release all those pent-up emotions. Assure them that the anger is a normal grief response.

Understanding: As humans we desire to fix things. We want the pain others are experiencing to go away, so we try to problem solve. Thus, we say to the widow, "You can remarry," and to the grieving parent, "You can always have another child," or "God never gives us more than we can handle." In supporting a loved one, remember the death of a significant loved one cannot be minimized by a replacement.

Allow a mini-life review to take place. Let them talk about what was finished or unfinished business. The time spent with the dead person was good, and life now is good also. Help them understand that what they are experiencing is normal, that they are not crazy, just grieving.

After someone has died, some examples of appropriate things to say are: "What I always liked about Joe was......," "I'll never forget the time he and I........," "May I take the kids to the beach today?," "It's OK. Tell me again about Mary," "I just phoned to say hello," "Tuesday will be a tough day for you. May we spend it together?" "I thought you might need a hug or someone to hold your hand today," "You don't have to hide your tears." Or, "I'd love to trim the bushes. May I do it for you?"

It is not easy to be a friend to a grieving loved one. It is painful, hard work. Yet, the reward comes when renewal in the bereaved becomes evident. Giving ourselves to a grieving friend or family member may enable them someday to give to others.

When I asked Barb Wheeler how she helped family and friends to get through the loss of a loved one to suicide, she told me one of the hardest things for those left behind is to finalize the death. In a normal expected death, you are able to finalize together. In a suicide, you do not get a chance to finalize the death together. "There is a lot of anger, because it was a lousy thing to do to those left behind." As Dr. Pilkington put it, "There is a lot of unfinished business when a person dies from suicide. My wife and I had time (three years) to take care of unfinished business, but my father's suicide left unfinished business behind."

"To help the family finalize," Barb said, "sometimes it would help to write a letter to the person who died to express their feelings. Other times, I would have them go to the cemetery to talk to the person to express feelings. Sometimes they just needed to express their anger toward the person. To finalize, the survivors need to develop a plan to go on with their own life." According to Dr. Pilkington, "Finalizing is a must, but forgiveness is another factor. We can forgive them for leaving us with unfinished business. We can forgive them for doing suicide."

The survivors may have questions like, "How will we function without this person?" or "What will the future be like?" "The survivors need to go on and make a life with the person no longer in it," Ms. Wheeler said. "I would give them resources in case problems came up. Within the family, the communication lines need to be open on any problem. Family meetings where each person gets to talk for 15 minutes without being interrupted may be helpful. Each person may choose to say or do whatever they want during their 15 minutes."

"Survivors of a suicide victim must know that it is OK to talk about it. Suicide is not a dirty word. It may be easier to talk about it with people who have been through losing someone to a suicide themselves. Many cities have S.O.S. groups, Survivors of Suicide, which may be very helpful to people.

"For survivors of suicide, many times, the hardest thing is the desire to know the reason why the person took their life. Unfortunately, nobody will ever be able to give them the reason why, because the only person who really knows is dead. There are usually many factors involved when someone completes suicide, not just one."

Don'ts in Counseling the Griever

> ➤ Support FLIGHT – moving, vacation, significant changes. This strips the griever from supportive family surroundings.

> ➤ Allow the griever to remain isolated.

> ➤ Let your own feelings of helplessness keep you from helping. You must be patient with the griever.

> ➤ Encourage the typical grief responses such as "don't cry," "don't feel guilty," "everything is OK."

> ➤ Avoid mentioning the person who has died.

> ➤ Let your needs and perceptions determine what the griever's grief should be like.

> ➤ Try to explain what happened in religious terms. "It was God's will" or "God needed them" will just make the griever mad at God. (Bichekas, Georgia, 1987)

In time, you may need to push them into a new world with your support. There will be times of "anniversary reactions"—birthdays, marriage dates, Christmas, Valentine's Day, and so forth. There will be flash backs of occasions spent with the lost loved one, making those occasions difficult to enjoy, especially the first year after the death.

"How Our Friends Helped After a Death to Suicide"

Knowing that I was writing this book, my mom and dad came across an article dealing with suicide that they mailed to me in case it was of any use to me. It is from the November 1999, issue of the *Eucharistic Minister*, and is written by Victor M. Parachin. The following stories and information came from that article and were reprinted with permission from Victor M. Parachin.

"Any death is devastating but a loss to suicide brings it's own unique pressures on the surviving family. How do you comfort someone whose loved one chose to take his/her own life? Here, in the words of surviving family members, are some ways that friends have helped when there was a death to suicide."

> *Friends came as soon as they heard of the death.* Immediately after the police notified Joyce that her husband, Jack, had taken his life, she recalls thinking: "His death shocked me, and the manner of his death was unthinkable. How would I tell the children? Who should I call? How would we ever get through this? Joyce says, "My family and I made it through Jack's suicide only because a whole community of comforters soon went to work on us." Within five minutes of hearing that Jack had ended his life, a friend was at Jack's home. "By nightfall of that day, 20 or 30 people had congregated at our house," she recalls. The friends included adults, teenagers, neighbors "we hardly knew." People hugged, talked, cried and even laughed. "Despite the horror of the day, these people affirmed life. They filled our home with their voices, their bodies, their food and we knew we were not alone."

> *Some friends came but did not say a word.* Often, just being there can turn out to be the strongest supportive factor for someone dealing with a suicide death. After learning his wife ended her life, Daniel called Rod, his best friend and jogging companion. "Rod came to the house immediately. He didn't say a word. He just came to me with open arms, embraced me tightly. I could see tears streaming down his cheeks. He couldn't talk but there was nothing to say anyway. For a moment I clung to him and cried as well."

> *Friends helped in practical ways.* One family was swamped with fresh flowers and plants shortly after friends learned of the father's suicide death. "Those flowers and plants symbolized life and hope for us," a family member shared. Other people ordered pizzas and sodas while others sent over casseroles. Neighbors started a collection for the family in memory of their father. "The financial gifts were greatly appreciated as our

family had many unplanned expenses because of the death. The children needed new clothes, a funeral had to be paid for and flowers had to be purchased," said the wife.

➢ *Friends attended the funeral.* Even though the death was suicide, people rallied around and came to the funeral service. Janice, 23, whose younger brother took his life, recalls being touched at seeing her church completely filled as extended family, friends, neighbors, colleagues and even strangers came to provide support. "Even the choir loft was full," she said. "One couple was in the choir but they were not regular choir members. They told me, 'We didn't know what to do, but we wanted to do something. Then we thought, *We can sing!*' So they sang. The presence of so many people at the funeral was a powerful reminder of love for our family," Janice says.

➢ *Teenage friends visited and made a difference.* Upon learning that a friend's husband ended his life, a woman went to visit. She brought her two teenaged children along to be with the teens whose father took his life. "On the way my children were awfully quiet but once they arrived they connected with the grief stricken teens. Soon they all began chatting and even laughing. My friend later told me that the presence of young people brought vibrant life to the house that day.

➢ *Friends prayed for us.* Via the mail, one family received the following scripture passage, which was carefully scripted in fine calligraphy: Even to your old age and gray hairs I am he, I am he who will sustain you. I have made you and I will carry you; I will sustain you and I will rescue you. (Isaiah 46:4) Included was this brief note: "I am so saddened by what has happened. Please know of my love and support for your family. I am including all of you daily in my prayers, certain that God will sustain you day by day."

➢ *Friends listened to us.* "Sometimes the greatest sermon is silence. A suffering person doesn't need a lecture, he needs a listener," notes Billy Graham. People who have a death to suicide suffer a harsh blow. They experience a variety of confusing and conflicting emotions such as anger, guilt, regret, loneliness and shame. They need people around who will just listen without offering advice and without judging their feelings. "Fortunately for my husband and me, we had friends who knew how to listen compassionately," says Sandy whose

19-year-old daughter ended her life. "Our friends let us take the lead in conversation. Instead of making assumptions about how we were feeling, they allowed us to talk and share our frustrations. Even now, nearly a year after the death, we have friends who just let us talk and talk and talk. The repetition seems to diffuse the intensity of our agony."

➢ *Friends did not allow me to withdraw from life.* After many years of treatment for depression, Robert's wife ended her life. "When the funeral was over, I began to retreat from life and withdraw from friends," he recalls. "That was a mistake which my friends would not allow me to make. For months after the funeral those good people visited and phoned regularly. They constantly invited me to various events and outings. That love and support was so gratifying and so enriching as to defy description. That caring continues to stand out in my mind as a bright spot in an otherwise bleak scenario."

➢ *Our friends continued to stay in touch.* Yvonne, a pediatric nurse and nursing instructor in California, has seen her share of dying children. Although she comforted many parents in their grief, she says nothing prepared her for the suffering she experienced when her son committed suicide. However, her friends were present when the news of the suicide was first made public and, two years later, they have continued to keep in touch with Yvonne. "At first, 'our closest friends were with us, and they were helpful in that they just listened. People still call and say, 'We were just thinking of you,' and 'How are you feeling?' A lot of people remember that February is hard for us."

It is easy for me to relate to each one of these stories, as we were fortunate enough to have been blessed with all of the things described by these families. There were so many people at Troy's Rosary and funeral, the entryway to the funeral home and church were full. They packed as many people into the pews as they possibly could. We received numerous plants and flowers, symbolizing life that we had to spread the plants among the family. We received a lot of food and casseroles at the house; so, I did not even have to think about cooking for quite some time. I even received two bags of groceries from a friend containing "necessities" so I would not have to go grocery shopping. Many friends and relatives stopped by the house to express their sympathies. The families in our neighborhood took up a collection in order to send a memorial. We received an incredible number of cards expressing sympathy and money for memorials.

My nephew, Ryan, was just under a year old at the time, so obviously he did not understand what was happening, but he put smiles on our faces as he entertained us. Troy's sister Tracy was the first person that I can remember actually making me laugh the day Troy died. It was not that she was being disrespectful or that she did not care about what happened, and I cannot even remember, anymore, what we were laughing about. I think it was something funny that Troy had done that she was reminiscing about, because I can remember going from crying to laughing. It was the most therapeutic thing I had done all day.

Many people and several church communities prayed for us. I had great friends who just listened when I needed to talk, without passing judgment or trying to tell me what to do. One high school friend used to stop by my house to see me about once a week, just to visit and to see how I was doing. Many of my other friends included me in things to make sure I was not just sitting at home thinking about my troubles. On the day of the five-year anniversary of Troy's death, we received two "Thinking of You" cards, one from my very good friend, Amy, and one from Troy's mom. The one from Troy's mom said how proud she was of us and that she loved us. The one from Amy, I actually received while she was on vacation in California. She had planned it in advance and made sure it would be mailed from her work so it would arrive at my house on the anniversary date.

So, as you can see, we have had a tremendous amount of support from family and friends, helping us get to where we are today. We would not be doing as well as we are without all of that love and support. Sometimes people have a tendency to want to handle things on their own without anybody's help, but life can be so much easier and happier if you accept help from others when it's appropriate.

Guidelines for Grievers

Another source of guidelines for grievers I received from the Methodist Employee Assistance Program. They adapted this information from *How to Survive the Loss of a Love* (Colgrove, Bloomfield, and McWilliams, 1976).

> ➢ **Recognize the loss:** It has happened – try not to avoid it.

> **Accept the grief:** To feel pain after a loss is normal. Do not try to be "brave." Express and honor personal feelings.

> **You are not alone:** Loss and grief are universal – everyone experiences them.

> **Talk about your feelings:** Share your grief with others. Talk with those you trust.

> **It's OK to feel depressed:** Take time to be sad and to cry.

> **It's OK to feel angry:** We all act angry over a loss – learn to channel it wisely.

> **Take care of yourself:** Eat properly and exercise regularly.

> **Keep busy:** Plan your days – activity will give you a sense of order. Avoid over-activity.

> **Seek comfort:** Accept support from others. Be gentle with yourself.

> **Reaffirm your beliefs:** Take advantage of your faith – lean on it.

> **Postpone major decisions:** Expect your judgment to be clouded for a while.

> **Keep a journal:** Put your thoughts on paper – it is a good way to let your feelings out.

> **Be open:** Give yourself opportunities to meet new people, places, ideas and experiences, but don't forget to build on the past. Don't discard what has been worthwhile to you.

> **Give yourself time to heal:** The greater the loss – the more time it will take. Never compare yourself to another grieving person.

> **Expect relapses:** There will always be things that trigger sadness again – this is normal.

> **Always maintain hope:** You will survive your loss.

Chapter 11

Put Your Life In God's Hands
Faith Will Help You Through It

When Troy died, there were lots of issues going through my head initially about how we would get through the difficult times that I knew were ahead of us. How would I help Jon and Natasha through this? How would I survive so I would be capable of helping them? How would we face the world again? How would I ever get over the guilt feelings, knowing that the primary reason he completed suicide was because of the separation I wanted?

One thing I did not even think about, however, was money. I knew we had a life insurance policy; so, I felt confident we would be OK financially. The majority of the money from the policy would be put away in Jon and Natasha's college funds, and we would use what we needed from it to survive. The possibility of not collecting on the policy did not even cross my mind.

Reality set in, however, when someone mentioned that we might not collect on the policy because his death was from suicide. Still, I thought, I would receive the benefits. How could a life insurance policy that we had been paying premiums on for quite some time not pay out when the person died? I did not remember for sure where I had stored the policy and did not want to think about it those first few days while we were planning and attending the funeral, so I put it out of my mind.

The day after the funeral, everyone had to go back to their own lives. I anxiously, but somewhat reluctantly, searched for the life insurance policy. My heart sunk and I felt faint as I read the clause about a "waiting period" for a suicide. In other words, you could not just go take out an insurance policy to provide for your family and then complete suicide. The "waiting period" was two years. Unfortunately, we had purchased the policy 1½ years earlier, so we would not receive the money from the policy. I thought to myself, "How are we going to pay the bills?"

135

God will take care of us, I thought. I kept trying to convince myself that somehow, some way, we would make it, but I was not so sure.

I was having a hard time believing this could be happening. Somehow the insurance company would feel sorry for us, or there would be some exception so we could receive our money for the life insurance. I was in denial. I could not believe the policy would not be available! So, I got on the phone and called the office where we had purchased the policy. I told the representative that Troy had died. He expressed his sympathies, and said they would get the paperwork going as quickly as possible. I said, "Then it will pay out?" as if he knew the death was a suicide. He said, "Of course it will," followed by a slight hesitation on the other end of the phone as if he sensed what had happened. Then he asked how Troy died. When I told him it was a suicide, he expressed his sympathies, and said he would have to check when the policy was issued. He told me about the two year waiting period, which I already knew about.

I also knew when we signed the papers for the policy, and it had not been two years. But I still kept hoping that somehow the date on my paperwork was wrong, or that there was something they could do to be able to pay at least a partial payment on the policy. He went to their files and found out the policy had not been in effect long enough. When he returned to the phone he said, "I'm very sorry, but there is nothing we can do." I was devastated. "The policy will, however, pay back the premiums you have paid in since it was issued," he told me.

This was at least a ray of light through the darkness. At least there would be some help to cover the cost of the funeral and burial. I did not even know what these costs would be yet, but I was sure it would be in the neighborhood of $7,000 - $10,000.

I knew we could take out a loan to pay for the funeral and burial, but thinking beyond the funeral, how would we cover everyday expenses? How would we pay the house payment every month? I had a good job and made good money, but I knew it was not enough to pay the bills we had at the time. So what were our alternatives? The first, most obvious thing that came to mind was to sell the house and buy a less expensive one. But the last thing I wanted to do was cause any more disruptions for Jon and Natasha at that time. Their lives had been shaken up enough, losing their dad, and I did not want to pull them out of the house and neighborhood they had lived in for several years as well, at least not for a while. If I had to sell the house, I wanted to wait at least six months to give them time to feel stable before I uprooted them again.

So how would we get by until then? My younger brother who lived in the same town as us at the time was single and making a good living. He offered to help out financially until we got back on our feet. Normally, I would never take a handout from someone, and I know he did not think of it as one. I have always taken pride in being able to make it on my own, without assistance from anyone. In this case, however, I was willing to allow Brian to help us through this tough time until I felt Jon and Natasha would be comfortable with a move to a different house and neighborhood.

After all of my worries about how we would survive financially without uprooting my kids from a comfortable environment, several things happened. I had forgotten about a $5,000 rider insurance policy I had on Troy where I worked. It was the maximum I could insure him for through work at the time. This paid for the majority of the funeral and burial, and the check I received from the other insurance company, for the premiums we had paid in, nearly covered the rest, which took a huge weight off of my shoulders not starting out with that debt. We also received an overwhelming amount of money in donations from family and friends. So I was able to pay the balance of the funeral and burial costs with money to spare to give donations in Troy's name.

While I was still in the process of trying to figure out where the money would come from to pay the house payment each month, and before I knew I would receive what I needed to pay the funeral expenses, someone mentioned checking into Social Security. I had not even thought about the possibility of receiving Social Security. I had always thought of Social Security as something you received after you retired. I did not know my kids or I might be eligible to collect this. In some respects, I felt like accepting Social Security was a handout, but I needed to do what I had to do to keep the kids in a stable environment, so I made an appointment to find out what they might receive.

I was shocked at what I found out. Previously I had only heard negative things about Social Security; that it was going away, that I should not count on it for my retirement, that it was not that much money anyway. So, I was hoping even to get $100-$200 a month from them to help pay the bills. After answering all of the questions, I sat on the edge of my seat as I watched while the Social Security representative entered the information into the computer to make the calculations as to whether or not Jon and Natasha were eligible for any benefits, and if so, how much. Once everything was entered and calculated, the printer began printing our fate. I held my breath as I looked down at the explanation laid in front of me. I shook, nervously, as I read what their benefits would be. I was ecstatic with the number I saw, and asked, "So is this how much Jon and Natasha will receive every month, or in a year's time?" She said, "That is how much EACH of them will receive every month." I turned and looked at my mom, who had gone with me for the appointment, and smiled the biggest smile I had since learning of Troy's death. I tingled all over as I breathed a huge sigh of relief that we would be able to survive financially.

In looking at the amount each of them received individually, it definitely would not have been enough money to live on if you were retiring on that income. However, it was more than enough to help us pay our monthly bills. In fact, I was able to put more than I ever had before into savings accounts for their college funds. Today, the majority of the money goes into those accounts. In fact, when I get a raise at work, I try to increase the amount deposited into their accounts. My ultimate goal is to eventually put all of the benefits received from Social Security into their college funds.

To find out more about Social Security benefits you may be eligible to receive, contact your nearest Social Security office or find them on the Internet at www.ssa.gov. Brochures, such as **_Survivors Benefits_** (Publication No.05-10084) and **_Social Security: Understanding the Benefits_** (Publication No.05-10024) would be helpful to read.

I guess Social Security is Jon and Natasha's "compensation" for having lost their father. There is no doubt in any of our minds that they would rather have him back than to have the money they receive from Social Security, but since we cannot make that happen, at least they will be able to go to whatever college they choose to go to. I have told them this is a college fund, not a new car fund.

I also encourage them to do their best in school and to get good grades. If they receive academic or sports scholarships and make it through college not needing all of the money in their college funds, then they may do whatever they please with it, but I will control the money until they have paid for their college. That comes first. I want them to learn the value of working hard to earn something for themselves rather than expecting someone to just hand everything to them on a silver platter.

The moral of this story is that God did take care of us. We went from wondering how we would pay the monthly bills and living from paycheck to paycheck, to being able to donate money in Troy's name to both of our high schools, Jon and Natasha's school, both of our churches we went to while growing up, and a new soccer complex that was being constructed at the time. I firmly believe that if you give to your church, synagogue, and so forth, and to other people in need, your donations will come back to you.

I had thought about writing a book for a while, but I was concerned about the effect it would have on Jon and Natasha. In August of 1999, while my kids and I were talking, I mentioned that some day I wanted to write a book in an attempt to help other people get through what we have been through. I was not sure how they would react to this and had thought I would probably wait until they were out of high school before I did anything about it. But once I saw their reaction, I knew I would not be waiting that long. I will never forget the looks on both of their faces as I told them what I wanted to do. They each had big smiles and their eyes were as big as saucers while they listened to me talk about my dream to help other people.

Jon said, "That's really cool, Mom!" and Natasha said, "Yeah, and we can help you remember stories about what happened!" Then Jon said, "So you're going to do this when you retire, when you have time?" He knew there was no way I had time to do this while trying to keep up with the schedule we already had. With me working full time, and then activities in the evenings, when would I get this done? He was right and I knew it.

I made the decision right then and there that I was NOT going to wait until I retired to write this book. I was going to do whatever I had to do and make whatever sacrifices I had to make to achieve this dream. So I started looking into the possibility of a leave of absence from work. I knew this would be a major financial strain, as there would be no income other than the Social Security for the kids, and we could not survive on that. I would have to take out a loan just for us to be able to live. I investigated the possibility of changing to a part-time status at work for a period of time, but I knew there was a chance they would not allow me to do this since a friend of mine had asked to go part time after her second baby was born, and they did not allow it based on the responsibilities of her job.

But that was a chance I had to take. I was bound and determined to write this book, and I knew I would do whatever I had to in order to get it done. I waited until the time was right, and I talked to my supervisor about it. He was very excited and supportive of my aspirations. I was going to be changing my job responsibilities in the near future, so because of the timing, since I would not be as heavily relied upon initially, he thought it would probably work. He presented the option to the management team of our department, and they agreed that it would be fine. Upon a suggestion from my supervisor, I had the payroll staff give me an estimate of what my take home pay would be if I dropped back to four days a week at the same pay level per hour. Due to the fact that I wasn't eligible to contribute to our 401k program after changing from full time to part-time status, the effect on my take home pay was not as drastic as I thought it might be. The bottom line is it really didn't matter anyway, because I had already made up my mind that I was going to make whatever sacrifices necessary to do this.

I was determined after all I had been through, to help others who are coping through the loss of a loved one to suicide. I did not care what I would have to do to accomplish this. I just knew it was what I wanted to do. I knew that sharing my story would help others, and it would help in my own healing as well. Helping others is very rewarding to me, so I would feel as though I had done the best I could in dealing with my husband's suicide. I encourage you to do whatever it is that would make you feel like you are helping others. Whether that is through writing a book, starting a support group, or simply participating in a support group, any way you can help others will be rewarding to you also. Participating in a support group will help you, but it also helps others to have someone to talk to who can relate to their feelings.

The next step for me to be able to write this book was to talk to people in Human Resources and find out what my options were. I was firm on changing to part time. All that was left was the paperwork to make it happen. My plan was to pay all of the monthly bills just like any normal month. The credit union where I work already had an account set up to automatically take out a loan to cover any overdrafts in my checking account. So I talked to a credit union representative about letting this loan build up as needed and paying it off after I was finished writing the book. I knew this would be stressful for me, because I do not like the feeling of not being able to cover normal expenses. The only time it seems appropriate to have a loan is for a major purchase, such as a car or a house. But I told myself to be prepared that this loan would build and not to get stressed over it because once the book was written and I went back to work full time I would pay it off.

So, I was prepared, the paperwork was done, and I changed to a part-time status as of November 1, 1999. Once I set my mind to the fact that I was writing this book, it took 2½ months to take drastic action. The first paycheck that would be affected, though, would not arrive until November 25, so at first it did not even feel like I was part time. But when it did arrive, I was pleasantly surprised by the amount I would be bringing home as a part-time employee. We could make a few cutbacks and almost make it on this salary. When the paycheck for the first half of December arrived, however, it was much smaller. "How could this have happened," I thought, "I must have done something wrong on my timesheet." Then it hit me. I had been a salaried employee ever since I graduated from college, so I had forgotten what it was like to be hourly. Since I was now part time, I was being paid for only the hours I worked rather than a flat rate no matter how many days there were in the pay period. And the timing could not have been worse, my last paycheck before Christmas!

I told myself not to get stressed if the credit union had to transfer money from the loan account to cover me that month. After all, I had planned for that to happen. Much to my surprise, we made it through that month without any loans being created! So I was feeling really good about the effect my change to part time would have on our finances. Since I didn't think we had changed our lifestyle any in order to reduce our expenses, I wondered, "How did we come up with enough money to pay the bills this month?" This just reaffirmed my belief that as long as we are giving to church and to others and living life the way we should be, God will make sure we are taken care of.

I also think that believing in some form of higher power, no matter what it may be or what religion, just the belief in a higher power, is helpful in our healing process. I remember several times after Troy died when Jon or Natasha would ask me a tough question; one that I was not sure how to answer. Sometimes I would think hard and come up with an answer for them, and sometimes it just felt as though the words were fed through me. Words came from my mouth at times that I did not know where they came from. As I heard myself responding, I would think, "Wow, that was good." I would simply look up and say, "Thank you, God, for helping me with that one. I could not have done it without you."

"Love comes to those who still hope

even though they've been disappointed,

to those who still believe,

even though they've been betrayed,

to those who still love

even though they've been deeply wounded before."

Author Unknown

Several times during my journey to write this book, I have had doubts about what I was doing. Was it really going to help anyone, or was I only dreaming? Would I hurt anyone in the process? Because if I did, it would not be worth any benefits received. Was my work really any good? Would anyone want to read it?

"Doubt is a pain too lonely to know that faith is his twin brother."

- Khalil Gibran

I was very fortunate that every time I started doubting what I was doing, I always had someone there to pick me up, brush me off and tell me that everything would work out. I had several friends who continued to encourage me when I doubted myself and my work. The other thing that kept encouraging me was that several times, things just seemed to fall in place for me. The way I found Dr. Pilkington to review my work was quite coincidental, and the fact that he agreed to do it before he had even met me in person was even more amazing. He had no idea who I was when I called him and asked this monumental favor of him, and he turned out to be a Godsend to me. He was a constant encourager who kept me excited about the project and believing in myself throughout the entire process. Everyday when I arrived home from work, I would run to the mailbox in hopes of receiving an envelope containing his feedback, and then I would delve into his comments like a little kid with a box of candy.

The way I found Barb Wheeler was also very odd, and she was quite helpful. And, the writing went much easier for me than I ever dreamed it would, with the entire project taking months less than I expected. There were numerous coincidences that could have easily not worked out for me, but did. When I shared these "coincidences" with Dr. Pilkington and Barb Wheeler, the response from both of them was, "It must have been meant to be."

When I was near completion of my writing, I had major concerns about the effect this might have on Jon and Natasha, and on Troy's family. I was so concerned about it that I was ready to cancel the entire project, even though I was almost done. I asked God to help me figure out whether or not this was the right thing to do. I also asked that if it was, to help me have the strength to finish, and if it was not, to help me have the courage to quit. About that time, a major break came my way in regard to getting published, and I had my answer. I believe God was telling me that I was supposed to do this, and that I needed to follow through with it. Since that time, I have not doubted the project, because I now have faith that it is what God wants me to do.

Our Christmas Gift to Troy

In 1998, prior to Christmas, I received an e-mail message that really touched my heart. It was written by a woman whose husband did not like Christmas because of the way society has twisted the meaning of it from the birth of Jesus to a materialistic, money-spending, hectic holiday where all kids think about is receiving gifts. One year the woman had an idea of the perfect gift to give to her husband. When Christmas day came, there was an envelope placed among the branches of the tree with his name on it. Inside was a letter to him explaining that she had donated uniforms, shoes and headgear to a wrestling team their son had wrestled against who obviously did not have the funding to purchase the proper attire. That was his gift that year, the donation to the wrestling team. Each year the woman found a needy family or group of kids to donate something to as his gift, and each year the opening of the envelope on the tree was the most precious and anticipated gift of them all, even for the kids.

After reading this, I was inspired to do something for someone and to make that our Christmas gift to Troy. Jon and Natasha thought that was a neat tradition also, and I hope to keep the tradition alive. This year we were able to donate boxes of groceries and several gift items to a young mother who had just left an abusive situation with her six-month old baby. This was during the time when my paychecks had just become smaller due to my change to part-time, but if I had to cut any corners at Christmas I did not want to cut this new tradition we had just started. I wanted to teach Jon and Natasha that Christmas is not just about receiving gifts. We should be in the spirit of giving, especially to those who are less fortunate than we are. I want them to realize how fortunate we are to have the things we have and that not everyone is as lucky as we are. I used to get depressed by the amount of money I spent at Christmas, but I have found that it really feels good to give to others.

This year Natasha went with me to drop off the items we had purchased for the young mother and her baby. On the way home, she said, "It feels really good to be able to help somebody else." That was the best Christmas

143

gift I could have received from her. I knew she understood what I was trying to teach her about the importance of helping other people.

If there is one thing I have learned from our experience with Troy's suicide, it is that everyone goes through difficult times in their life, but they survive through the help and support of others. As Jesus says in the Bible, "Do unto others as you would have done unto you." I had many people who helped me, and my kids following Troy's death. Now I would like to give back by giving to families who are struggling, whether financially, or with a suicide death of someone close to them.

Reading the Bible

Every night when it was time for Jon and Natasha to go to bed, it seemed like there were always excuses, last minute things that needed to be done, and it took at least a half-hour from the time I would tell them it was time for bed to the time they actually got there. Also, many times after they went to bed, I would hear them talking to each other even though they did not share the same room. It was not uncommon for me to yell from downstairs for them to quit talking and get to sleep. One night it was taking them an extraordinarily long time to get to bed, and I could hear them talking in their rooms. I quietly snuck up the stairs and found them whispering in Natasha's room by the light of the closet. "That's it!" I thought. I had told them to stop talking and get to bed, and here they were still up. They were REALLY in trouble now. I was going to give it to them. Quickly, I turned the light on, ready to pounce like a lion after his prey and say, "I caught you!"

Eyes wide, they looked up in surprise, scared because they had been caught... caught reading the Bible! Natasha had her First Communion at church a few weeks earlier, and I gave her a children's Bible which they enjoyed reading. Normally, we say prayers before Jon and Natasha go to bed, but that particular night it was getting late, and I wanted them to get to bed so we skipped our prayers. Since we skipped our prayers, they decided to get out the children's Bible and read a story from it. Here I was, ready to reprimand them, and here they were, reading a story from the Bible. I swallowed hard with a lump in my throat when I realized I was about to scold them for reading the Bible. My tone changed in a hurry as I told them to simply finish it up as quickly as they could in order to get to bed.

I felt guilty. It had been my choice to not say our prayers that night because there just wasn't time. It had been a test of faith that I failed, and my children passed. It has been through their strong faith in God and in guardian angels that they have dealt with their father's death in such a healthy manner. And that is one philosophy of theirs that I do not want to change.

The Little Girl

I would like to share another story I received recently through an e-mail message about a little girl. It was titled "AND THE LITTLE CHILD SHALL LEAD THEM..."

There was an atheist couple who had a child. The couple never told their daughter anything about the Lord. One night when the little girl was five years old, the parents fought with each other and the dad shot the mom, right in front of the child. Then, the dad shot himself. The little girl watched it all.

She then was sent to a foster home. The foster mother was a Christian and took the child to church. On the first day of Sunday school, the foster mother told the teacher that the girl had never heard of Jesus, and to have patience with her.

The teacher held up a picture of Jesus and said, "Does anyone know who this is?" The little girl said, "I do, that's the man who was holding me the night my parents died."

I believe God will come to us and help us in our time of need if we will only allow him into our lives.

Do You Believe In Guardian Angels?

As regular church attendees and believers in God and an afterlife, Jon, Natasha and I also believe in angels. Having faith and belief in a higher power is a great coping mechanism and stress management strategy. We were very fortunate that even though Troy was in enough misery that he could take his own life, he was not selfish enough to want to hurt us intentionally.

On the morning he died, before he left, he had talks with Jon and Natasha separately. As I lay in bed, I could hear bits and pieces of their conversations. For the most part, I heard a lot of crying. Troy was crying because he knew what was about to happen, and that this would be the last time he would see or talk to his kids. Jon and Natasha were crying I'm sure mainly because Troy was crying. I doubt that either of them had ever seen him cry before. I thought he was telling them good-bye because we were separating. Little did I know he was telling his kids good-bye for the last time… forever.

I vaguely remember overhearing him ask the kids if they believed in guardian angels. They have told me since then that he said he would be the best guardian angel they could ever have. They, of course, did not understand what he was telling them at the time. While I was overhearing these conversations, I was very distraught over what was happening, and I was not thinking clearly. It did not register in my mind either what he was trying to say. I thought he was trying to tell them that no matter what, even when he could not be with them, he would be watching out for them anyway.

I am very thankful to Troy for having had those conversations with Jon and Natasha. As I look back on the time since he has been gone, I believe it has helped us on numerous occasions. It has helped Jon and Natasha to know that their dad loved them very much because the last words he spoke to them was a promise that he would eternally be looking out for them and watching over them.

There have been many times when we have had close calls, like the speeding trip to the airport I described in Chapter 6, a near accident, and so forth, when we have looked at each other and said, "It's a good thing Daddy is watching over us!" This helps us always remember Troy in a positive light. Even though he is gone, he is still doing good things, especially for us.

Shortly after Troy died, I remember one night when Natasha was walking around with a pillow on top of her head. I told her to put the pillow back where she found it. Then she explained to me that she was carrying Daddy. She had gone into my bedroom and taken his pillow off of the bed. As she carried it on her head, she believed she was carrying him with it. He was an angel, of course, so he was not too heavy for her to carry. I never again tried to stop her from carrying a pillow on her head.

What Do Angels Look Like?

Like the little old lady who returned your wallet yesterday.

Like the taxi driver who told you that your eyes light up the world when you smile.

Like the small child who showed you the wonder in simple things.

Like the poor man who offered to share his lunch with you.

Like the rich man who showed you that it really is all possible, if only you believe.

Like the stranger who just happened to come along when you had lost your way.

Like the friend who touched your heart when you didn't think you had one.

Angels come in all sizes and shapes, all ages and skin types. Some with freckles, some with dimples, some with wrinkles, some without. They come disguised as friends, enemies, teachers, students, lovers and fools. They don't take life too seriously, they travel light. They leave no forwarding address, they ask nothing in return. They are hard to find when your eyes are closed, but when you choose to see, they are everywhere you look.

So open your eyes and count all your angels, for you are truly blessed!

- Author Unknown

I do believe there are real-life angels all around us every day. Mrs. Stranberg was an angel for us, Jon's sixth grade teacher, and all of the teachers at St. Isidore's, were angels, Karen Kelly was an angel for me while I was healing, Dr. Pilkington was an angel for me while I was writing, and all of our friends and family have been angels for us over the years. We just have to look at people as angels. We need to see the angel in those around us instead of only looking for the bad things about others.

The first summer after Troy died was Jon's first year he was old enough to play baseball. I will never forget one of his first baseball games. I was assigned the duty of "passing the hat" in the crowd to collect money to support the baseball league. I was to perform this duty halfway through the game. I had watched every play of the game until that point, but while I had my back turned to the field as I passed the hat, I heard cheers from everyone in the stands. Jon had been playing third base, and when I turned around in response to the crowd's reaction, I saw him throw the ball back to the pitcher. I was told that he had made a fantastic catch on a line-drive hit to his right side. His first great play, and I missed it!

After the game, when we got into the car to go home, Jon asked me, "Did you see my good catch, Mom?" My heart sunk as I told him how disappointed I was that I had watched every play up until that point, but that I was busy collecting money from the crowd when he made the catch. His head slowly dropped to his chest as he said, "I just wish Dad could have been here to see it." Tears welled up in my eyes as I had thought the same thing to myself. I knew Troy had seen his catch, but I wished he could have been here to tell Jon what a great catch it was, to give him a hug, and to look him square in the eyes and tell him how proud he was of him. I told Jon, "He DID see that catch, and he saw every play you made and every hit you had, because he has the best seat in the house. Instead of sitting in the grandstands with obstacles to block his view, he could see the game better than anyone that was actually there and I guarantee you, he was VERY proud of you!"

As Jon and Natasha get older, they are both involved in a lot of activities. It is getting harder and harder for me to be at all of them. Many times they have games or tournaments at the same time, so I cannot be in both places, but they always understand. They know that I do the best I can to be at as many of their games as I possibly can. They also know that whether I can be there to support them or not, they always have a very big fan observing, because Troy is watching them from above.

Jon, Natasha and I would also have group hugs. I love hugs, especially from my kids, and Natasha was always good about initiating a group hug. If one of us was crying about something, or happy, or just felt like a hug, she would always want to include everyone. She would say "Group hug!" and the three of us would huddle up. One of the first few times we did this after Troy died, we were standing there hugging, and she said, "Be careful, you're squishing Daddy!" We spread our arms a little further apart in order to make room for Daddy in our hug.

Natasha, carrying Daddy around on her pillow and including him in our group hugs, was probably triggered by the talk Troy had with her about being her guardian angel. Even though he is not here with us physically, he is here with us in spirit. This was a very healthy way for us to deal with him not being with us, because in a sense, he still is with us. For Natasha, it was probably like having an imaginary friend, only her imaginary friend was her dad. As long as she understood the reality that he actually was gone and that he was not coming back, at least she could think of him as being with us in spirit.

Natasha received an angel desk calendar one year for Christmas from her Godmother, Troy's sister, Tami. I thought it was pretty neat since Tami lives several states away from us so we do not get to see her very often, and I do not think she knew that we think about Troy as our angel. It was a perfect gift. Natasha loved reading the daily sayings about angels. One night as I kissed her good night, I read the angel quote for the day.

"Sure-footed, silent steps march with us along the paths of our lives: the steps of our guardian angels."

Holiday (NZ)

Troy is with us in spirit every minute of every day as our guardian angel. I would like to share another poem I have received about angels.

I found a penny today

Just laying on the ground,

But it's not just a penny

This little coin I've found.

Found pennies come from heaven,

That's what my Grandpa told me,

He said Angels toss them down

Oh, how I loved that story.

He said when an Angel misses you

They toss a penny down,

Sometimes just to cheer you up

To make a smile out of your frown.

So don't pass by that penny

When you're feeling blue,

It may be a penny from heaven

That an Angel's tossed to you.

- Author Unknown

I love the penny story, as again it proves that everything in life is all in how we look at things. I never used to waste my energy to bend over and pick up a penny. A nickel or a dime, I might pick up if I was not in too big of a hurry. A quarter I would definitely pick up, but not a penny. Ever since I read this poem, when I see a penny on the ground, I smile and think of it being tossed down to me from heaven. I stop, back up, pick up the penny and put it in my pocket.

I received the penny poem shortly before Christmas one year and I shared it with Jon and Natasha. On Christmas Eve, as we were preparing the weight bench in the garage, which I had bought for Jon, I glanced down on the dirty garage floor and saw a penny. I smiled, picked it up, rubbed it off and put it in my pocket. It was as if Troy was telling me he was there with us at Christmas.

Chapter 12

It's Your Choice

Become Stronger or Let It Consume You

While attending an International Toastmasters Convention held in Chicago in August, 1999, I had an experience that I will not soon forget. I noticed a gentleman who carried a walking stick and wore dark glasses. As much as I tried not to stare, he stood out in the crowd because he was "different." My curiosity was roused, as he didn't appear to have been blind since birth. I was interested in finding out his story and what happened to him. He lightly touched the shoulder of another gentleman, who led the way in front of him. Otherwise he appeared to be quite proficient, as if he knew what he was doing from having navigated before, with full sight, and without any assistance.

At the conclusion of one of the educational sessions, my friend Carolyn and I struck up a conversation with these two gentlemen who had been seated in front of us. Allan and his cousin Vince turned around and introduced themselves, which is a very common thing to do at a Toastmasters Convention. I noticed immediately that Allan reached out to shake hands as he introduced himself, and appeared to almost "see" what he was doing.

We discussed what everyone's plans were for the evening. Carolyn and I had planned to eat at Harry Caray's, and we invited Allan and Vince to join us if they would like. We decided to meet in the lobby of the hotel at 7:00 that evening. Once everyone had arrived in the lobby, off we went to walk to Harry Caray's.

From the minute I met Allan, I was curious how he lost his sight, but did not feel comfortable asking. I wanted to analyze the situation first to make sure Allan was comfortable talking about it. As we walked, it became obvious that he was. He joked about his visual impairment numerous times and made several matter-of-fact statements about it. It was clear that he handled the entire situation of his loss of sight with incredible grace. So, when the time was right, I finally asked him what had happened.

I listened intently as he told his story. When Allan was two years old, one of his cousins was carrying him on his shoulders through a wooded area. As his cousin made his way through the trees, a branch flung back like a rubber band, off of his cousin, and into Allan's eye. This caused the loss of sight in his left eye.

Despite this, Allen triumphed. He was voted "Best Offensive Lineman" of his high school football team and was the captain of the wrestling team. He was on top of the world and living life to the fullest, when in his mid-20's, while innocently driving under a bridge in Kentucky, he was shot at from above in an apparent drive-by shooting. At this point, as Allan told his story, he lifted a tuft of hair off of his forehead and showed us where the bullet had grazed him. He explained to us that, as the bullet hit his forehead, it exploded, and a piece of shrapnel flew under his glasses and into his right eye. This shattered the retina, thus the loss of sight in his right eye.

The odds of any type of accident to cause a person to lose sight in one eye are very slim. But the odds of experiencing two tragic accidents, years apart, separately causing the loss of sight in each eye, has got to be astronomical! I was shocked and impressed with how eloquently he handled his misfortune. He made people around him at ease with it due to his obvious acceptance of the situation.

As I got to know Allan better in the next day and a half at the convention, I told him how in awe I was with his adaptation. He said, "I didn't deal with it very well at all at first. For two and a half years, I laid on the couch doing nothing but letting my hair grow out, feeling sorry for myself, and contemplating suicide. Finally, I got to the point where I realized that even though my sight had been taken from me, my life had not. It was time for me to start living that life again."

The last evening of the convention, I shared with Allan my experience with the loss of my husband to suicide, and the desire I had to write a book about it. As we parted ways I told him, "I am so impressed with the way you handle the loss of your sight. I don't think I would deal with it as well myself." He said, "I'm sure you would, and I am equally overwhelmed by how you have coped with the loss of your husband." I smiled at him and said, "You know, none of us really know how we will react to something until it actually happens to us."

Ultimately, we make a choice as to how we respond to things that happen to us in our lives. We have the freedom to make the best of things or to sit around feeling sorry for ourselves and expecting everyone else to feel sorry for us as well. We can become stronger because of our choice, or we can simply melt away into nothing like the wax of a burning candle. If we elect to drown in self-pity, we will remain bitter and unhappy as long as we continue to make that choice.

However, we can change our choice at any point in life. Allan started out with the choice of self-pity. Through the love and support of family, he decided he did not want to live that way any longer. He made a new choice to accept his loss and make the best of his life. Since that decision, he met and married a beautiful lady, Cathy, and together they have two beautiful children, Alexandra and Allan, II.

In a matter of two days, Allan and I became great friends as we shared our stories with each other, and gained a tremendous mutual respect in how we had each met with and triumphed over our very different, but difficult situations. Allan taught me an important lesson about growing stronger, and was an example of courage and the strength to persevere.

Allan and I have kept in touch, and he still amazes me as he talks about all of the things he does in his life. Some of these things are probably things that some people WITH sight have never done. But Allan doesn't let his loss of sight stop him from doing anything. He doesn't use it as a crutch or an excuse for not being able to do something. In fact, sometimes it's hard for me to believe that he is really blind. He sets a great example for all of us that we can do whatever we set out to do in life if we just believe that we can and never give up.

We are all given mountains to climb in life. Some of us need better climbing equipment than others, and each of us may need different climbing equipment to climb one mountain than we do for another. In one case, we may need sophisticated equipment to climb the mountain, such as a harness, backpack, rope and the appropriate shoes for scaling steep cliffs. This equipment could be compared with counseling to provide security and to comfort fears and risks associated with conquering our own mountains of denial, guilt by association, confusion and blame. Climbing mountains requires a tremendous amount of strength and endurance, but reveals great beauty once the feat is accomplished and we stand at the top of that mountain, victorious. When another mountain is placed before us, we may be able to scale the side of the mountain with our bare hands.

One critical piece of climbing equipment for all of us is choice. We all make choices as to how we will climb the mountains placed before us in our lives. We can sit at the base of the mountain, convincing ourselves that it is too steep or too difficult to climb, so we never try. We then must watch while others scale that mountain and experience the joy from having met with and conquered the challenge. Or, we can be one of those standing at the top of that mountain with our fists held high in the air, shouting, "Yes, I made it! I did it!"

Many people have told me how impressed they are that I am writing this book. I really do not think it is anything extraordinary, though. I believe that each and every one of us has the potential inside to be able to do what I am doing. The only boundaries we have are those we set for ourselves. It is only important that you respect yourself and what you are doing.

It is a choice that we make whether we will accomplish great things, or we will be content with what we currently have. In a speech given by a very good friend of mine, she asked us the question "Are you happy?" She said that she really does not like the word, "content," because content to her, means "average." It means being complacent and afraid to take risks, rather than striving to be all that you can be to achieve all of your dreams.

> **"Some people think that successful persons are born that way. I'm here to tell you that a champion is someone who has fallen off the horse a dozen times and gotten back on the horse a dozen times. Successful people never give up."**
>
> Jean Driscoll, six-time Boston Marathon Winner
> (Wheelchair Division) as quoted in *A Hero in Every Heart*
> by H. Jackson Brown, Jr. and Robyn Spizman

It is our choice how we will deal with the mountains life places in front of us. If we choose to work our way over them, we become much stronger from overcoming the adversities we experience.

As Larry Marik stated in his presentation, which was discussed in Chapter 3, "Significant emotional events are the only thing that can change our internal programming." I believe I have become much stronger and wiser because of what I have been through. I am a different person today than I was before Troy's death, and I do not think I would be where I am if it were not for the significant emotional event I experienced and the way I chose to deal with it.

"Wisdom is not taught, it comes from experiencing life."

Taken from the reading of *Celebrate the Sun*

One of Webster's definitions for wisdom is "knowledge and good judgment based on experience," and a definition for mature, is "fully developed in body and mind." I believe that wisdom and maturity have everything to do with the types of experiences a person has had, how they have handled themselves through them and what they have learned from them. Good judgment and the development of mind, has hardly anything to do with how many birthdays a person has had. Just because a person gets older does not necessarily mean they get wiser. If we don't learn from our experiences, we never get any smarter. We simply stay the same. Having birthdays makes us older, but not automatically wiser or more mature. Maturity has to do with understanding life and what's important in life. Sometimes I think my kids are more mature in mind than some of the adults I know. They have experienced a lot in their young lives, have handled it very well and have learned a great deal from it.

Many people go through life feeling sorry for themselves for things that have happened to them and never learning anything from their experiences or mistakes. This is sad, as they will never grow any stronger or wiser. What you make of your life is up to you. Your answers are your own. You can either GO through an experience, or GROW through it.

Jon IS Stronger

The first time I mentioned anything about my desire to write this book to Jon and Natasha, I explained that I would like to be able to help other people get through what we had already been through. Jon was in the third grade when Troy died, and Natasha was in kindergarten. They have both moved on now from the elementary school they went to when Troy died, to the junior/senior high school, which combined students from two elementary schools besides their own. Many of the kids in their new school do not know what happened to their dad. This was part of my concern with writing a book. The last thing in the world I wanted to do was to have any kind of negative effect on my kids. I knew this book could potentially stir up new questions from some of their friends who did not know them when Troy died. I didn't want to put either Jon or Natasha in an uncomfortable position. However, they were both very excited about the idea of me writing a book. When I told Jon that it may stir up some new questions from kids that didn't know him when his dad died, he just said, "I think I can handle it."

This made me feel that he is much stronger today than when this originally happened. Initially, he was grateful to his friends for being nice enough not to talk about it around him. Now he is prepared for people to ask him questions about what happened.

"Problems are only opportunities in work clothes."

- Henry J. Kaiser

Every time something negative or hurtful happens in our lives, we have an opportunity to become stronger if we are willing to work hard to get there. We have to look at our problems as opportunities, though, rather than feeling sorry for ourselves for what has happened to us. If we aim at nothing, we will succeed. But if we set our sights high, aim for something better than we have today, and are willing to work for it, we will be able to achieve the things we set out to accomplish.

Parent/Teacher Conferences

When I went to Jon's eighth grade parent/teacher conferences, I picked up his grade report with the list of teachers for his classes and made my way around the room to each of them. Since the conferences are held in an "open house" format in the school cafeteria, for grades seven through twelve, parents simply wait in line to talk to each of their children's teachers. Each teacher has a table, and it is chaotic and noisy as conversations are being held throughout the room. Chairs are sliding across the tile floor as one parent stands up to let the next parent in line sit down.

I had about three teachers left when I stopped at the junior high guidance counselor's table because Jon had a class with her. She was new to the school, so we had never met. I sat down in the chair across the table from her, and amid the chatter which filled the room, said, "Jon Scholz," so she would know whom I was there to discuss. Instead of looking through her stack of papers to find Jon's, she just smiled at me with a blank stare on her face. I looked around, thinking maybe I had gotten the wrong teacher, because it appeared as though she did not know whom I was talking about. After a few seconds of staring at me she said, "I've been waiting to meet you!"

My initial reaction was, "Uh oh. Has Jon been in some kind of trouble?" Especially since this was his guidance counselor. Then she went on to explain. Since it was her first year at the school, she did not know any of the kids. The first day she had Jon in class, she started going around the room asking the kids a little about themselves. She asked Jon, "So what does your dad do?" She said that he responded calmly, without hesitating that his dad had died. She felt terrible about having put him in this awkward position and thought she should change her approach. When she moved on to the boy next to Jon, she decided to ask him about his brothers and sisters. It just so happened that this boy had lost a brother in a tragic accident, so he told her that his brother had died also. This being her first year of teaching, she got broken in the hard way. She said she did not push for any more answers from Jon about what happened, because she did not want to put him in an uncomfortable position. She had been waiting to meet me so she could ask me what happened.

I told her Troy completed suicide, and that I had started writing a book about our experience. She was so intrigued by this that we talked for about a half hour, whereas most of the conferences with each teacher last about five minutes. It was comforting for me to know, though, that Jon handled the question in front of many new friends who had not known what happened, with ease. He did not show any signs of discomfort, he simply answered the question in a matter-of-fact manner. This confirmed what he had told me that he could handle it if the book brought out new questions from people. I also felt comforted that for the rest of his life, when he is asked: "… and your parents?" or, "What does your dad do?" or, "How are you like your father?" he will be able to answer those questions comfortably.

Since I started this project and people who know me have heard about what I am doing, I have heard stories of other people who have done something to make themselves stronger because of what they have been through. One woman who lost her husband from a suicide now helps with grief sessions at her church and is going back to school to learn more about counseling so she can help other people. Unfortunately, there are still people who have not dealt with their experience properly and are still struggling with it. I hope this book will help everyone who reads it in one way or another, meeting my objective. My hope for you is this.

"Comfort on difficult days,

Smiles when sadness intrudes,

Rainbows to follow the clouds,

Laughter to kiss your lips,

Sunsets to warm your heart,

Gentle hugs when spirits sag,

Friendships to brighten your being,

Beauty for your eyes to see,

Confidence for when you doubt,

Faith so that you can believe,

Courage to know yourself,

Patience to accept the truth,

And love to complete your life!!!"

Author Unknown

Sitting On Daddy's Lap

About a week after Troy died, the kids and I were loading the car to go to his mom's house. We had received so many beautiful plants from people that I could not keep them all, so we were taking several of them to his mom and grandma. We were also going just to spend the day with them. When Jon, Natasha and I would go somewhere in the car without Troy prior to his death, Natasha would sit next to me in the middle of the front seat, and Jon would sit in the passenger's seat. This was the first time the three of us had gone anywhere in our car together since Troy died.

As I loaded the car with the plants, Natasha opened the passenger door to get in. She jumped into the passenger seat, but rather than sliding over into the middle of the front seat like she normally would, she just sat there. As I stood by the car with the driver's door open, she looked over at me with a disgusted look on her face and said, "Mommy, Daddy won't move over!" You see, in her mind, Daddy was sitting in her spot in the middle of the front seat. My mouth dropped open, as I stood there dumbfounded, not knowing how to respond. I waited for God to help me with the words, but before I had a chance to formulate something to say to her, she let me off the hook. She said, "That's OK. I'll just sit on his lap!" and she moved over into the middle of the front seat.

Even at six years old, she chose to think of her daddy as an angel in her midst, rather than being consumed by feeling sorry for herself. I think we can all learn from her example.

I hope the choices Jon, Natasha and I have made, concerning how we coped with our loss, will help them be stronger when they are parents themselves. I also hope that sharing our story will help you better understand your own experience. May you choose to rise above the adversity of your loved one's death and scale the mountains which loom before you, knowing your journey will make you a stronger person. Have hope and belief that you can get through your difficult climb. I did. It was a struggle at times, but the view is much better at the top!

Bibliography

Bichekas, Georgia. "Bereavement" workshop, 1987.

Bichekas, Georgia. "Depression and Suicide" workshop, 1986.

Brown, H. Jackson, Jr., and Spizman, Robyn. *A Hero in Every Heart*. Thomas Nelson Incorporated, 1996.

Canfield, Jack, Hansen, Mark V., and Kirberger, Kimberly. "A Simple Christmas Card," *Chicken Soup for the Teenage Soul*. Deerfield Beach, FL: Health Communications, Inc., 1997.

Carewise article, 1999.

Cavanaugh, James. *Celebrate the Sun*. Dutton/Plume, 1973.

Cavanaugh, James. *There Are Men Too Gentle to Live Among the Wolves*. Dutton/Plume, 1970.

Colgrove, M., Bloomfield, Harold H., and McWilliams, Peter. *How to Survive the Loss of a Love*. Prelude Press, 1976.

Corey, G. *Theory and Practice of Counseling and Psychotherapy*. Pacific Grove, CA: Brooks/Cole Publishing, 1996.

Dinkmeyer, D. C., Pew, L. L., and Dinkmeyer, D. C., Jr. *Adlerian Counseling and Psychotherapy*. Monterey, CA: Brooks/Cole Publishing, 1979.

Dreikurs, R., Grunwald, B., and Pepper, F. *Maintaining Sanity in the Classroom; Classroom Management Techniques*. New York: Harper Collins Publishers, 1982.

Kubler-Ross, Elisabeth. *On Death and Dying*. New York: Macmillan, 1970.

Methodist Employee Assistance Program. *Helping/Counseling the Griever*.

Parachin, Victor M. "How Our Friends Helped After a Death to Suicide," *Eucharistic Minister*, edited by Joan A. Wingert.

Kansas City, MO: The National Catholic Reporter Publishing Company, November, 1999.

Redfield-Jamison, Kay. *An Unquiet Mind*. A.A. Knopf, 1995.

————-*Night Falls Fast*. Knopf: Distributed by Random House, 1999.

Sahler, Olle J.. *The Child and Death*. Mosby-Year Book, Incorporated, 1978.

Social Security Administration. *Survivors Benefits* (Publication No.05-10084). July, 1999

Social Security Administration. *Social Security: Understanding the Benefits* (Publication No.05-10024). January, 2000.

Tatelbaum, Judy. *The Courage to Grieve*. Harper Trade, 1980.

Touched By an Angel, television show, 1999.